Praise for *Pregnant with Hope*

"An excellent book! As an infertility specialist, I plan to recommend it to all of my patients as part of their ongoing care. I recommend it to anyone who cares for or about infertile couples."

Dr. Andrew Toledo, Medical Director
Reproductive Biology Associates
RESOLVE Hope Award Recipient

"Pregnant with Hope invites couples on a journey of hope and healing of the kind only God can give. This is a book for struggling couples, and for those of us who love them and often don't know what to say or do. I'm so thankful for this resource. May God use it mightily."

Dr. Stephen A. Hayner, President
Columbia Theological Seminary

"I love this book! We make it available to every couple experiencing a pregnancy loss, stillbirth or newborn death. It can be very comforting to those searching for answers."

Aimee Alexander, Director
Northside Hospital Perinatal Loss Unit

"Pregnant with Hope opens a door into what is often a secret world of dread and disappointment to call fearful couples into the loving heart of God. It is truly a gift—a guide through the wilderness of infertility to joy."

Ethel Ware Carter, Program Director
Regional Council of Churches

"Pregnant with Hope belongs on every therapist's bookshelf. It is an incredible resource for those working to foster environments in which lives are transformed and hope is found."

Todd Sandel, Executive Director
LifeGate Counseling Center

Pregnant with Hope

Good News for Infertile Couples

Susan Radulovacki

Servant's Heart Books

A division of Vinings Village Press

Servant's Heart Books
A division of Vinings Village Press
© Copyright 2010 by Susan Radulovacki

All interviews incorporated into this text are verbatim transcripts of conversations with infertility Bible study participants. Actual names are used.

Unless otherwise noted, all scripture verses are taken from the *Holy Bible, New International Version®*. Copyright © 1973, 1978, 1984 International Bible Society. All rights reserved throughout the world. Used by permission of International Bible Society.

Scripture quotations marked (NLT) are from the *Holy Bible, New Living Translation*, copyright © 1996, 2004, 2007. Used by permission of Tyndale House Publishers, Inc., Carol Stream, Illinois 60188. All rights reserved.

Scripture quotations marked (Message) are from *The Message*. Copyright © 1993, 1994, 1995, 1996, 2000, 2001, 2002. Used by permission of NavPress Publishing Group.

Library of Congress Cataloging-in-Publication Data
Radulovacki, Susan.
Pregnant with Hope: Good News for Infertile Couples/Susan Radulovacki.
—2nd ed.
p. cm.
ISBN 978-1-4421-3738-7
1.Infertility – Psychological Aspects 2. Infertility – Religious Aspects – Christianity 3. Christian life 4. Bible – Criticism, Interpretation, etc.
I. Title.
BV4509.R338 2010

Servant's Heart Books may be purchased in bulk for educational, business, fund-raising or other sales promotional use. For information, please contact VVPress@bellsouth.net or write: Vinings Village Press, 2849 Paces Ferry Rd., Suite 610, Atlanta GA 30339.

First Servant's Heart Books edition 2010
Printed in the United States of America
10 9 8 7 6 5 4 3

For Branko, Katie & Ryan.
I love you more than you can imagine.

For the glory of God.
You alone, Lord, make all things possible.

Contents

Preface

Although it ended years ago, I remember our infertility journey vividly. It seemed incredibly long and profoundly lonely. At the time, my husband and I kept our struggle secret. We knew of no one else going through the same experience–except the strangers we saw, month after month, in the doctors' waiting rooms.

We felt singled-out for suffering we could not understand. Trapped in a story we could not escape. None of it made sense to us.

I had grown up believing in a God who is generous, loving and faithful. Now, my faith was confronted with questions I could not answer: Why is this happening? Where is God in all this? Why are we suffering and struggling when it seems so easy for everyone else? When will we have a baby? Will we *ever* have one? What have we done to deserve this? What do we do with our anger at God? Our grief? Our fear? All of the other emotions we seem to be taking out on each other? And, how do we get our lives back without giving up on our dream?

Our church offered little comfort. Despite thousands of members, no one–neither pastors nor congregants–ever openly acknowledged the infertile couples in their midst. And sadly, none of us ever self-identified.

We were separated by our silence. Alone in our quest.

After the long-awaited birth of our daughter, I realized what an oppressive burden silence had been. At a gathering of new mothers, one woman self-consciously admitted that she'd used Clomid to stimulate ovulation. The floodgates opened. Within minutes, we discovered *all* of us had experienced infertility; no one had been able to conceive without help.

We had all made the same incredible journey—every one of us feeling isolated and alone. What a relief to break our silence and to realize that none of us had been singled-out for suffering. All of us had faced the same uphill battle.

In an instant, I saw that we could have provided one another such comfort and support, if only we had shared our secret. Instead, our silence had compounded our suffering.

At that epiphany moment, I promised myself: no more secrecy. I would share our story… any time, with anyone. I would do whatever I could to help other couples who were trying to conceive find comfort and community.

Over the past decade, I have fulfilled that promise—first, by training and serving as a Stephen Minister, and then, by leading a nondenominational Bible study designed specifically for infertile couples. This one-of-a-kind ministry offers couples a forum for wide-ranging discussions of the spiritual questions and relationship challenges that often accompany infertility.

If you joined us, we would welcome you—regardless of your faith tradition—and invite you to participate in our search for answers, and for hope. I would reassure you that the purpose for meeting with one another is to confront infertility head-on, to seek God in the midst of it, and to ask hard questions about whether the Bible has anything relevant to say.

The couples who have participated in the class have described their infertility journey as transformational. It no longer represents only suffering and loss. Through studies and discussions, they have come to see this period of their lives as a time of profound spiritual growth and preparation for their future as parents.

God may have the same plan in mind for you.

At the suggestion of those infertility alumni, and with the guidance of the Holy Spirit, this book was written to speak directly into your heart—as if you were meeting with us, and sharing your struggles with people who understand the journey.

Welcome.

Welcome

What is the best news someone could give you today? You're pregnant, of course. That would solve everything... wouldn't it? But chances are, if you've been struggling with infertility, God has something else in mind.

That can be an unsettling thought.

Would it help you to know what? And *why*?

You, along with six million other infertile couples (just in the U.S.), are part of the surreal world of infertility, combining high-tech science with profound uncertainty and extreme anxiety. The experience is certain to test your outer limits—and the strength of your faith in the promise that God will not give you more burden that you can bear [Psalm 145:14].

Be assured God has a purpose for you in this. You are free to choose whether to seek an understanding of that purpose, or to ignore His desire to redeem your experience. To that extent, you are in control. Which sounds like good news. But somehow, that alone is probably not enough to make you feel better.

Right now, worry, frustration and despair are consuming tremendous stores of emotional energy as you and your partner try to get out ahead of your problem.

Maybe you just need a better plan. Or a better doctor. Or better information. Or a better procedure. Or...*something*.

Will it ever happen? That's all you want to know. What if it doesn't? It doesn't feel safe to dwell on that. And where is God in all this?

Wrestling with infertility will shake the foundation of your relationship, and repeatedly test your commitment to the shared dream of parenting. It will expose your fears and exploit your vulnerabilities. It will challenge your faith head-on.

Whether you allow God to work in and through these circumstances will determine whether this becomes a period of spiritual growth for you, or simply one of intense, prolonged suffering.

● ● ●

Infertility will challenge your faith head-on

● ● ●

How do I know? My husband and I have grieved more lost children than we have been able to bring safely into the world.

The two who survived the process of conception and delivery benefited from our access to experts in reproductive medicine and neonatal intensive care. One underwent open heart surgery when she was just four weeks old. The other entered the world six weeks premature. He was briefly considered a candidate for brain surgery after just three weeks of life.

Their arrival—and survival—was miraculous to us, and life-changing. It was the fulfillment of a hope God had placed in our hearts long before. Long before the temperature-taking and ovulation-predicting, the daily injections and IUI's, the endless doctors' appointments and stressful waiting for test results. Well before we knew what a long-lasting, faith-challenging journey infertility would become for us.

Our first-hand experience with infertility, along with several other life-threatening challenges, brought us to tears—and sometimes, to our knees. But, thanks to those experiences, we came to know God as relentless and intentional in His pursuit of us. And, full of grace. We learned that He is neither reckless nor random; every life experience has a purpose.

Over the course of a person's life journey, God can transform loneliness and despair into intimacy with Him, heartache into wisdom, and seemingly tragic life events into the path to joy. *If* we will allow Him to.

That's why I began leading a Bible study for infertile couples. As a Stephen Minister, I have been trained to comfort people suffering through life's most difficult challenges. And as an infertility alumna, I am familiar with the journey infertile couples are facing.

In reading and discussions, our groups have confronted deep doubt about God's faithfulness, issues of suffering and feeling separated from His love, questions of judgment and condemnation, and fears of hope dying along with embryos.

● ● ●

This is a haven for hurting souls seeking much more than commiseration

● ● ●

We've provided a haven for hurting souls seeking much more than commiseration. Every couple arrives hungry for spiritual wisdom and understanding that reaches soul-deep. They acknowledge fears and admit failures in search of spirit-sustaining hope. They need a God-centered, faith-based reason to believe it will happen for them. And God delivers.

Week after week, we cross through territory filled with emotional and psychological land mines. Ultimately, we arrive, transformed by the journey, in a promise land of new hope.

This book was written to welcome *you* into our discussions—to bring you comfort and insight into the reasons for a season of infertility. That understanding can bring you peace. And hope.

You will not hear reasons as the world defines them: "because you have an ovarian cyst," "because the sperm count is abnormally low," "because an STD caused irreparable damage." Instead, we'll discuss God's reasons: because He loves you, because He has an incredible child to entrust to you—when you are ready, because He wants to give you His best.

God longs to use your circumstances for your benefit. The potential has been created; the opportunity exists. And, the Bible says He will – if you will let Him [Romans 8:28]. So, approach this book with an open mind and a willing spirit. Each chapter will deliver news of God's goodness and faithfulness deep into your heart. This will strengthen you for your journey.

Realize that, as you read, you may feel an instinctive need to guard your heart. That's because infertility often brings with it a sense of vulnerability, and an impulse for self-protection. Remember that your presence here is part of a divine appointment. This book was written for *you*. It's a gift from the God who loves you and will protect you. So, you can lower your defenses and still be safe.

The world's need for pretense falls away in our group discussions. We all know the struggle isn't easy. So, instead of pretense, we offer acceptance—of you, your spouse, and the way things actually are. There is no judgment. No second-guessing. Only love, and grace, and encouraging good news.

The other souls who are reading this book are your journeying companions. Like you, they are en route to a future as parents. It may feel, initially, as if you've been forced to join a sad little club. But in truth, these strangers are destined to become incredibly committed parents. Like you, they care deeply about the role they're longing to play. Even if you never meet or talk with them, find comfort in the knowledge that *you are not alone*. They, too, are on this arduous journey.

You may choose to seek out other couples who are struggling with infertility—to form a group that can approach this book in a structured, intentional way. Or, maybe you prefer to protect your privacy—to read and think alone.

Either way, plan to commit your mind, your heart and your spirit to interacting purposefully with these lessons. Give yourself over to the process as completely as you can. Trust that God is at work—that He has a specific purpose for the time you spend with these ideas.

Anticipate questions appearing in each chapter, almost

● ● ●

Find comfort
in the
knowledge
that you
are not alone

● ● ●

like speed bumps, *to slow you down*. Take the time to consider each one of these. They will help you dig deeper and understand more of what God is trying to reveal to you through this experience. The questions will also keep you from racing ahead, as if finishing this book quickly could somehow speed your passage through infertility.

It can't. And unfortunately, it won't.

In fact, one purpose for this time of waiting may be to *slow you down*, to teach you to wait for God.

However you choose to proceed—urgently or with patience, alone or with others—know that the Holy Spirit meets you here…to comfort, to strengthen, to guide. Christ promised he would be with you always [Matthew 28:20].

Trust that the longings of your heart and the cries of your spirit will be heard as you make your way through these lessons. Try to approach each one with grateful anticipation, trusting that—ultimately—this will be a life-giving and hope-sustaining journey.

Shall we begin?

"… I am the Lord, your God, who takes hold of your right hand and says to you, 'Do not fear; I will help you.'"

Isaiah 41:13

Feeling Desperate

For many infertile couples, being on the receiving end of unsolicited advice is frustrating, and at times, insulting. Don't people realize that you have done your homework, read the research, and tried everything worth trying? Why, then, do they feel compelled to offer such patronizing wisdom:

"Relax; it's stress that causes the problem."

"Exercise more; your body needs it."

"Get some rest; it's all about fatigue."

"Quit thinking about it; that just makes it worse."

"Take a vacation; you'll come home pregnant."

"Tell him to wear boxers, not briefs."

"Adopt; you'll get pregnant immediately."

"Try not to worry."

And so on. By the time couples reach our group, they have already proven to themselves that Pollyanna prescriptions are useless. These modern-day myths and scraps of old wives' tales just rub salt in the wound of infertility. They do so by suggesting that solving the problem is as easy as following simple advice.

One reason friends and acquaintances offer advice so frequently is that it makes them feel better. People feel uneasy when they can't solve a problem for you. They want to offer help and hope, but they don't know what to say.

The best thing to offer would be genuine compassion,

but that would require them to be emotionally present with you in feelings of powerlessness and despair. For many people, that's too much to ask.

⚫　⚫　⚫

Other people's advice feeds our hunger for actionable hope

⚫　⚫　⚫

There's a reason infertile couples continue to give an ear to unsolicited advice, despite its consistent impotence. It feeds our hunger for actionable hope—for control in a situation that is utterly uncontrollable. Our desperate need to find the answer makes us vulnerable to any suggestion that holds the promise of forward progress.

Is that necessarily bad?

No, but experience quickly teaches us to be cautious—not to get our hopes up too high. Otherwise, we risk that familiar surge of this-could-be-it, followed by the stomach-churning ride to the bottom of the emotional roller coaster when we discover: It isn't.

It is *hard* to resist a new possibility, if only for the moment it takes to consider and discard it. Unfortunately, what looks like a clear direction to head out of the current circumstances, and on toward the dream, turns out—repeatedly—to be a mirage. Nothing more than false hope. Again.

With time and experience, infertile couples teach themselves to disregard most unsolicited advice in favor of scientific expertise. Reproductive endocrinology and high-tech obstetrics & gynecology hold out possibilities that myths and old wives' tales cannot. These solutions work well for some couples. But for others, the hope they offer is a more expensive, but equally elusive mirage. Not every couple responds to egg-stimulating drugs or IVF procedures. Worst of all, in many cases, no one knows why.

These experiences generate increasingly intense emotional roller coaster rides, and the cumulative psychological effect can be disorienting and devastating. Hopelessness feels increasingly unavoidable. Anxiety expands to fill the available space. Yet, couples refuse to relinquish their hold on the dream of becoming parents.

Is there any alternative? Any place else to look for help and hope?

When couples reach their limits or realize they are fast approaching them, they often feel drawn to our group. Whether the limit is psychological, emotional, physical, spiritual, or some combination of all four—they experience it as real, and their circumstances as unbearable. *Something* has to change.

⚫   ⚫   ⚫

Pause and consider (or discuss) this.... When people offer you advice about how to resolve your infertility, how does it make you feel? Do you sense yourself approaching a limit— either psychological, emotional, physical or spiritual? Do your circumstances ever feel unbearable?

⚫   ⚫   ⚫

The desperate desire to find the answer in, or for, ourselves is nothing new. Sarah, the first infertile woman mentioned in the Bible, was a wife and aspiring mother. God had promised her husband "a son coming from your own body who shall be your heir" [Genesis 15:4]. Sarah was impatient for a baby—or maybe she projected that impatience onto her husband. Either way, she wanted that child.

Maybe she grew tired of failing to conceive as others succeeded. Maybe she was fed up with useless advice. Maybe she resented the shame and isolation that accompanied her status as an infertile woman.

Whatever the reason, she elected to push God's promise from the future into the present by telling her husband to sleep with her servant. The Bible says she reasoned, "...perhaps I can build a family through her" [Genesis 16:2].

I can build.... I can... I'll have to....

Sarah had neither the will nor the faith to trust that God would build her family in time to meet her need. All thoughts were of failure and the desire to build a family *now*.

She did not seek God's blessing on her decision. In fact, she did not seek God at all. Nor did she ask her husband to, despite the fact that God had spoken to Abraham about children many times before.

> Sarah did not seek God's blessing on her decision; in fact, she did not seek God at all

According to the Bible, she consulted no one. She trusted only herself, and her plan. She made a decision and communicated it to her husband with the imperative: "Go, sleep with my maidservant."

Sarah's helplessness and impatience were overwhelming. She had reached her limit. Something had to change—fast. So, she took the initiative to change it.

Sarah's plan succeeded. Her servant conceived—but, resentment was born. The servant resented Sarah. Sarah resented her husband. When Sarah laid the problem at her husband's feet, he handed it right back to her: "Your servant is in your hands. Do whatever you think best" [Genesis 16:6]. So, Sarah mistreated the servant—who ran, taking the pregnancy with her.

•   •   •

Pause and consider.... Can you relate to Sarah's feelings of impatience and isolation? Can you understand her desire to press for a solution, even if it means compromising her dream?

What about Abraham? Can you understand his response to the situation as it spirals out of control? As Sarah looks to him to "fix" it? Is the pressure he feels familiar to you?

•   •   •

This nightmarish chain of events was not the intended fulfillment of God's promise to Abraham. Time after time, the Lord had reiterated His promises, making absolutely clear His intention to bless Abraham and Sarah with a son. But they could not wait.

Desperate impatience is a common problem for infertile couples. Left grasping at straws, we are willing to try almost anything to conceive. Anything but waiting patiently for God's timing. *That* requires a deeper level of faith than we can muster in the midst of this relentless pursuit.

Right now, there must be something we can do, or aren't doing, that will speed up the process. We've got to get busier, push harder! The desire is so strong, the dream is so powerful, we feel as if we have to do whatever we can to make it happen.

Do you recognize yourself in Sarah? Or in Abraham?

Sarah built her hope on faith in her capacity to conceive. When she realized she couldn't—and concluded she wouldn't—her faltering hope told her it was time for Plan B. Her impulsiveness, her impatience, and her intensity are all understandable. And also, very familiar.

Infertility brings with it a set of temptations that are irresistible—the greatest of which is: trust your perceptions over God's promises. Meaning, if you sense He has forgotten you, He has. If you sense He will not bless you, He won't. If you sense it's time for action, it must be. If you sense you're on your own, you are.

Sarah trusted all those perceptions.

Abraham followed Sarah's lead. He accepted her decision without question or protest. He didn't seem to consider the consequences to his relationship with her, or worry about the servant's decision to flee (taking his child with her).

He balanced Sarah's controlling behavior with accepting acquiescence. No insight was ever offered; no alternative was

● ● ●

Sarah's hope was built on self-reliance, rather than faith in God's goodness

● ● ●

proposed. He did not remind Sarah of God's faithfulness to their ancestors, or His many promises to give Abraham more descendants than could be counted [Genesis 13:16, and 15:5]. Instead, he gave in to the same temptation Sarah did—to trust his perception of the situation more than God's promise.

●   ●   ●

Pause and consider.... Do you recognize any aspect of your infertility experience in Sarah and Abraham's? Does her choice to push—or his to acquiesce—mirror yours? What does that indicate to you? Might their story be relevant?

●   ●   ●

When we tell ourselves we have full responsibility for our success, and work to establish complete control, we leave very little room for God. Believing a baby will come only by our action, thanks to our persistence, if we never stop trying... is to enthrone ourselves. We do it out of fear that God is nowhere to be found.

Sarah was not wrong to want a baby; God intended to make her a mother. Abraham was not wrong to respect his wife's needs; God intended to meet them. But Sarah's scarcity thinking would not let her wait. It prevented her from trusting God.

●   ●   ●

Pause and consider.... What does "scarcity thinking" mean to you? Is it an apt descriptor of your current mindset? How might that be affecting your ability to trust God with your infertility? With your dream of becoming a parent?

●   ●   ●

Despite Sarah and Abraham's lack of faith—and lack of patience—God did not break His promise. He did not punish

Sarah or Abraham for their choices. The servant's son was born, safe and healthy, after she returned to Sarah and Abraham to make peace. Sarah got what she thought she wanted—or what she assumed Abraham wanted. But the Bible says nothing about joy.

For the thirteen years that followed, God was silent. Over time, Sarah accepted her chosen fate: her husband had an heir—the son of the servant—and he would inherit all they had. This reality fell far short of the promises God had made, though.

When life is hard, we are tempted, like Sarah, to assume that God is absent—or worse, utterly unconcerned. The opposite is actually true. The Bible says we can assume He is using our circumstances as a "spiritual refining process" that is preparing us for the gift He intends to give [I Peter 4:12, Message].

● ● ●

When life is hard, it's tempting to assume God is absent or unconcerned

● ● ●

Rather than ignoring or punishing us, God is allowing our experiences to mold us in anticipation of the blessing He has planned. The gift that *is* coming.

In the case of Sarah and Abraham, God used the 13-year period of silence to cool Sarah's feverish obsession. He waited for her to recognize she was powerless to create the joy of a son conceived with Abraham. He waited for her to accept her human limitations, and to (re)gain humility. When this process was complete, she was prepared to receive the gift He longed to give: the seed of God-inspired hope.

God wanted more for Sarah and Abraham than compromise, followed by resignation. So, when Sarah finally let go, God rebooted the story. He began again, right where He had left off—"A son is coming to you, Abraham"—and He added, "Sarah will be the mother" [Genesis 18:10].

Sarah overheard and could hardly believe it. Hope, alive again?! When she laughed at the prospect, God asked Abraham,

"Is anything too hard for the Lord?" [Genesis 18:14]. One year later, the answer was clear. Ninety-year-old Sarah delivered a son whose name, Isaac, means laughter.

It is human nature to feel desperate when we can't see a solution to a problem that will not leave us alone. And our desperation can sometimes lead to pointless, self-destructive or irrational acts.

Even when it doesn't, it can create a black hole of despair that makes it hard to think clearly, or hear God. Truth be told, we know that we are not omnipotent or omniscient. Infertility forces us to face these limits, like Sarah, and then find a way to live with ourselves.

Naturally, we are tempted to push harder, as Sarah did—or to acquiesce, like Abraham. In such moments, it helps to remember that waiting for God is an act of faith.

● ● ●

It helps to remember that waiting for God is an act of faith

● ● ●

Periods, even moments, of *in*action are a way to say "yes" to God's implicit questioning: Will you wait for Me? For My best? For My perfect timing? It is a difficult choice to make when we confuse busyness with staying hopeful, or frenzied activity with making progress. So, sometimes, our circumstances must make clear that waiting for God is the only choice we have.

God used the 13 years of waiting to prepare Sarah—and Abraham—for the blessing He had planned all along. The blessing He had *promised*. He used their circumstances to create a sense of impossibility and set the stage for something miraculous.

Having reached their limits, they stopped hoping in their ability to bring their dream to fruition. That opened the door to a new kind of hope, based on God's promise and His faithfulness.

God created that seemingly irrational hope, planting the seed with such detail that it eliminated any possible explanation but grace: the longed-for son, conceived by his two parents, would be born in less than a year [Genesis 17:21]. Impossible? And yet, it happened exactly as God said it would.

Might it be that God is using your circumstances to prepare the way for a miracle? Do you believe that could be possible? Do you believe He even cares?

Can you imagine a hope that is not self-reliant?

Does the God of the Old Testament, who proved Himself a promise-keeper, have anything to offer you in your current circumstances?

This is where we begin our Bible study—searching for the promise-keeping God of scripture, in hopes of finding a message as compelling to us as the promise of hope He gave Abraham and Sarah.

Reflections

This page is for you. Use it however you like—to journal, to jot notes, to capture insights or list questions… whatever will help you connect what you've just read to *your* infertility journey.

_____

_____

_____

_____

_____

_____

_____

_____

_____

_____

_____

_____

_____

_____

_____

_____

_____

_____

_____

_____

Michelle & James

The opportunity to share stories with other infertile couples is one of the great blessings of our Bible study. Couples begin to sense walls of separation crumbling as hopeless isolation is replaced by genuinely supportive community. To enable you to experience that blessing, ten couples agreed to share their stories in their own words....

Michelle & James, how did your story begin?

Michelle: We met at 28. James moved here from New York to start a business. I was recruited to come work for a company. Someone invited me to their church, and I met James there.

James: We were both in a singles' Sunday school group.

Michelle: We dated for a year and a half. Then James asked me to marry him at a private dance lesson. That was fun. He got down on his knee in front of the instructor, who happened to have a camera....

We had a six-month engagement, and then got married. Traveled the world. Lived our lives. They were full—very full.

We always knew we wanted a family, but we never really talked a lot about it. So, I was starting to track my cycle and I realized things weren't happening. I went to my OB, and he put me on Clomid. Still, there was nothing happening. James was kind of in denial.

After 2½ years, things were not moving quickly enough with my OB. He suggested I might need surgery and I didn't want to do that, so I initiated meeting with a reproductive endocrinologist.

James: Michelle and I were on different planets, I guess. I knew we were sort of trying, but I didn't realize we were *trying* trying for a couple years.

In my mind, it was: if it happens, it happens. It was important to me, but it wasn't like, this is what we need to do—have a baby. That was more her thinking and I was just going with the flow. Which was fine for a while. I thought it would work out. If it's meant to be, it's meant to be....

Michelle: "If it's God's will..." you'd say.

James: I was very casual about it because it's a scary thing to think about being a parent. We were only engaged what... six months? That's pretty quick.

Michelle: I think typically men are slower than women to respond on certain things. I don't mean to be stereotypical, but I think women have a maternal instinct—and maybe men don't follow the same timing.

So, month after month, we had no success. False pregnancies. No positive pregnancy tests. I had one friend who was going through infertility. She was really my rock and my resource because I had no other idea what to do or how to do it. She was the one who was really encouraging me and guiding me. That's how we ended up with the doctor we went to.

James: The pressure built up more for me as we started to go to a doctor, and then we started to find out all about possible complications, and options, and... it was like, Whoa! This is a lot more serious than I thought.

Month by month, we did different tests and procedures.

Pressure really started to build—and now, there was more urgency. When I felt that pressure, I guess I pulled away. Meanwhile, Michelle wanted to communicate more.

That's a very typical man-woman response. She wanted to talk more; I wanted to go do some yard work and decompress. That's when a lot of stress built up in our marriage.

Michelle: We started to go to therapy.

James: Therapy was great for us to learn more—about each other...

Michelle: ... and about our own ways of grieving. We learned we had very different ways of handling the fact that we had friends having one child, onto their second child, and we still had empty arms.

It was hard for James if we were at a Sunday school event and there would be daddies pushing their little children on swings and he'd be standing on the deck, watching. Or me, going to baby showers and different events. It was hard!

Therapy opened my eyes to realize James was a team player and he *was* supportive. He was as hurt by this—and grieving as much about it—as I was. The first time we started talking about it in therapy, he cried. And he's cried multiple times since then, because it is very sad.

James: Before, I'd be like, "I can't deal with this. It's too much to handle. I have my own issues with this." Which wasn't fair to her. For me, the solution had been to go do something else, go fix something else. But that can really tear up a marriage.

We learned in therapy that you need to listen to your partner. Listen and be supportive—then they can get it all out and feel better. Michelle's pressure would be relieved somewhat, and then I'd feel better, too.

It's so hard. Everybody's got kids and everybody's just perfect. It's Beaver Cleaver. Everybody says, "I've got my two kids and my dog and everything's just great." It's like a weight on you.

Michelle: At this point, God was not part of our journey. We were trying to do it under our own power. It was hard because I was so intensely focused on the medical part of trying to get pregnant. And at a reproductive clinic, all you do is have tests and meet with doctors, week in and week out. I know that He was with us, alongside us, grieving with us... but we didn't invite Him to be part of our whole journey.

We didn't want to go to church anymore because of the grief of seeing baptisms, or Mother's Day and Father's Day. We couldn't do Sunday school when all they do is talk about their kids. There was really no place for us. We felt like, "Why is this happening?" I didn't understand why.

James: I sure came close to being angry at God. I didn't understand at all. And you come to that point where you think it can't get worse....

Michelle: The whole thing was really stressful. I traveled a lot for work at the time, so trying to synchronize all the tests and shots and medicines and everything else.... It wasn't intimate and it was affecting our marriage.

James: There was other stress, too. Our golden retriever got cancer. During her chemo, I couldn't go near her stools because of the radiation—I could become sterile. But I had to gather samples for the vet. So, I had to be extra careful with this radioactive poop, wearing gloves....

Michelle: At certain points, we just lost the ability to think clearly. We were on our way to visit my family and it was time for James to give me an injection in my stomach. Those shots were over $1,000 each. The syringe dropped on the pavement. I looked at James and said, "Just pick it up and put it in."

Thank God my uncle was there because he said, "You cannot put that needle in you."

I said, "You don't understand! That's like $1500 dollars on the ground!" I picked it up and said to James, "Let's use it." It was really intense, wasn't it?

James: Yeah. We really needed a break.

Michelle: We decided we would try going to a Christian therapist and see if that might bring our faith into it. We only went once because, in all fairness, I don't think he could've done what we wanted him to do. We had to learn how to incorporate the Lord into our lives on our own. He couldn't do that for us.

James: A lot of people who have nothing left, they go to God.

Michelle: When all else fails, go to the Lord… and we should have gone to Him from the beginning! But, He's very patient.

James: When everything's great, you can feel tempted to put God in the bottom drawer. We started to get closer to God and give it to Him, and that's when…

Michelle: … God said, "Oh, Michelle and James. You have finally come to the realization that I have been with you all along. You're being obedient now."

We went to the church and said, "We're struggling! We feel so isolated. We need help. There's no place for us to go. There are all these groups, but where do we fit in? We don't fit in anywhere. We're not single, we're not married with children… we're childless."

We knew we weren't the only couple in this enormous church with infertility. There had to be others who were struggling like we were struggling, and felt alone, like we felt. We wanted to start a Bible study. We wanted to grow in our faith so that we could understand why this was happening, that we weren't alone, and so we could build community with others.

The church agreed to help us.

We needed to promote the new Bible study, so people

knew about it. So, the communications director interviewed us and the church published an article about our infertility journey.

James: That felt great to me because it felt like we were reaching out to help other people with what we were going through. It felt good to be part of a group that could help people have discussions on infertility issues, and answer questions about Christianity.

Michelle: I was scared to death of no longer being anonymous. I was an executive and I didn't want the whole world to know about something as private as our infertility journey. But now, it would be known by anyone who read that newsletter. At the time, the church membership was close to 12,000—so that was pretty huge. For me, that was really scary.

James: It felt good to me. The spotlight was definitely on us because it was a story about our personal experience, but it felt like getting a weight off my back to get it out—and hopefully help other people. I felt pretty good that this might help us all out, somehow.

Michelle: About that time, someone at the church indicated there was a woman with a prayer group that met in her home; I could consider calling her. So, I did. I started going a month before the Bible study started. That's when my faith started to deepen and my walk started to fast track a little bit.

We were scheduled for a frozen transfer on September 18th. Earlier that week, James' mom called me and told me to watch the 700 Club. I'd never watched the 700 Club before—it was a little too radical for me. But that particular morning, my mother-in-law said to find out when the 700 Club would be on; I needed to watch it. That's all she said.

So, I sat down and watched with my dog.

The co-host was praying, so I bowed my head in prayer at the same time, and then she said, "There's someone by the name of Michelle who's watching right now. She is like Sarah.

And she needs to know that she will have a child very soon."

I opened one eye like, Did she just say that? I called my mother-in-law back and asked, "Did you call this in?"

"No!" she said—she didn't. She told me when they heard the co-host say, "Michelle is going to have a child...," their mouths hit the floor.

I called James at work. For him, it was surreal. Of course, why wouldn't we believe it...?

That was a complete turning point for me in my relationship with Christ. I literally got on my knees crying like you cannot believe, "Lord, I'm giving it to you. There's nothing more I can do. I've done all I can. It's all about this Type A personality. Me-Me-Me. Control. Control."

I realized it wasn't in my power to have a baby. It was all His. And I gave it to Him that day. Then Saturday, we had the transfer.

James: Right after we did our frozen cycle, I remember thinking, "I don't know what we're going to do if this doesn't work."

Michelle said to me—I remember this so clearly—"Negative thoughts and feelings don't come from God. They're from the enemy." That was a real breakthrough for me because I was letting the devil beat me up. He was winning! I was thinking all these negative thoughts and my views on everything were so twisted.

She said, "Let's focus on giving it to God and do what He thinks we should do." And I'll tell you... that really helped me.

Michelle: I remember being in the shower the morning of the first Bible study. I was praying and I thought, the Lord is going to bring the perfect group together. And He did. The community that came together was wonderful.

Some of the couples said, "Wow, we can't believe you shared your story." But we wanted to communicate that what you see when you go to church every week isn't real for every single couple. *Everyone* has issues.

This was our intimate issue, and we knew there were others out there with the same intimate issue. We did what God wanted us to do, really.

James: Then, we got the news.

Michelle: Yes. The second class, we were scared to death to announce that we were pregnant. Here we were, wanting to join in with these people and be on the journey together—we'd had failed IUI's, a failed IVF, a frozen cycle—and then, success: a twin pregnancy.

We told the group—and they were elated!

It made us realize that, in that environment with other couples on the same journey, it's a different feeling when you hear that someone's pregnant. You're joyful and hopeful because you know it can happen for you, too.

What did you learn from your infertility journey?

Michelle: I learned a lot through this journey. My relationship with Christ has grown exponentially as a result.

James: If we'd put God front and center sooner, it would've been easier. Sweating bullets for so long, and then having Him there, has just made me stronger as a Christian.

Michelle: I would do it completely different now. The Lord was with us—but if I could do it again, I would be talking His ear off from the beginning, not waiting so long to invite Him into our journey.

James: With infertility, your faith is on the line because you're praying about it, but there's that thought: "What if we don't have children? What if we're going to be miserable like this...?" You've given it all to God, but is He going to provide?

Michelle: Infertility took us to a different level with God. Not just individually, but also as a couple. As a very impatient person, I learned *a lot.*

You have absolutely no control over it. If we had learned that earlier on, things might've been different. But that wasn't God's plan. He wanted us to slog through the mud and the swamp, to trudge through it all. And then, to give Him the glory for the outcome.

I've grown past the embarrassment I sometimes felt admitting that I didn't invite the Lord into our journey earlier. Now, I'm sharing that story as often as I can because I hope it will help other people not fall into the same trap.

I believe the frozen cycle worked because of our obedience and faith, and because it was God's perfect timing.

Facing Defeat

Walking into our meeting room for the first time, every couple steps out in faith. They know they are leaving behind their initial hope for a "normal" pregnancy, along with the hopes that followed for a complicated-but-swiftly-successful one.

Now, they are seeking a new kind of hope. They need something that will equip them to face the future that awaits—and the fear of continued heartache that looms large.

For some couples, this is not an easy step to take. Their private pain will become public. Their sense of having failed at something hugely important will be impossible to deny.

The biggest hurdle, though, will be accepting that there is no going back. Joining the group means recognizing and accepting their current status as "infertile." Pretending that infertility is someone else's problem is a crutch that will no longer carry psychological weight. So, they must leave denial at the door, trusting that something better awaits them.

When they arrive, they find seats around the circle. There are often indications of suffering in body language. Many are deeply wounded by what they have already survived. Some have difficulty hiding their pain. Eye contact is enough to bring tears. Others send unintended signals of self-protection and avoidance: arms crossed, gazes averted, huddling close to their spouse.

There is some nervous small talk. But mostly, there is

silence and separation. *How did I get here?* is the question on every heart.

All of them have crossed a divide. A gaping chasm. They have left behind the world of everyone who seems to conceive without try-ing, or discovers it has happened when "we only started trying a few weeks ago!" That world, and all its inhabitants, feels incredibly distant—unattainable and painfully desirable.

Far from it, but still across the divide, is a much smaller universe of formerly-infertile couples who have succeeded in conceiving or adopting. Grateful for their new sta-tus, many of them lean into normalcy with enthusiasm, and delight in intentional amnesia. *Any trouble conceiving? That's behind us now.*

> *How did I get here?* is the question on every heart

• • •

Pause and consider.... Do you share the feeling of having crossed a divide when you acknowledged your current status as "infertile"? How do you feel about leaving your hopes for an easy, "normal" pregnancy behind? What else do you sense yourself leaving behind?

• • •

For the men and women who join this group, entering the community of still-infertile couples means acknowledging the truth: It isn't happening. And, more than that: Everything we have tried has failed—and we're not sure we have the emotional stamina to keep going.

Is that where you are now in your struggle with infertili-ty? Deeply invested in becoming a parent? Emotionally depleted by the process of trying? Tired of failing, of grieving, of loss? But, still unwilling to give up the dream nestled securely in your heart?

Every couple that chooses to set off on the journey with us makes a sort of mental calculation. They weigh the antici- pated emotional burden of confronting the truth of their circum- stances and their despair against the possibility of renewed hope. They recognize that they have not been able to "fix" their infer- tility; nor can I. But, they believe God may turn His heart towards them if they reach for Him.

It's worth a try.

●   ●   ●

The Bible promises, "Come near to God and He will come near to you" [James 4:8]. This spiritual axiom tells us that when we move, God moves. He responds to our choice to approach Him by approaching us. Our drawing near draws God nearer to us. It invites Him to be closer.

> The spiritual axiom tells us, when we draw nearer, God does, too

Simply by taking the step of faith to cross the threshold and enter our meeting room, couples create the potential for a new nearness with God.

●   ●   ●

Yes, it's a small step. But that one step of faith—indicating a willingness to open their minds and hearts to a new understanding of their infertility experience, in light of the Bible's truth—causes God to come closer.

How do I know? I have seen it happen with couple after couple.

Am I sure it will work for you? Yes, I am. The Bible promises that if you genuinely seek God, you *will* find Him [Matthew 7:7]. The deeper, more difficult question is, what do you expect to experience when you do? And does that make you more or less willing to "draw near"?

As you know, infertility can feel like an Old Testament curse on a household. It drives a wedge into otherwise healthy relationships, sows seeds of doubt and despair in hearts of faith, and creates a sense of suffering in isolation that seems boundless and unending. It makes God feel distant, unresponsive—utterly unmoved.

Is that a God you want to draw near to?

* * *

Pause and consider.... Does the idea of drawing near to God comfort you? Leave you ambivalent? Apathetic? Alarmed? What are those feelings based on? Can you imagine them changing—or has infertility simply reinforced them?

* * *

Consider this... what if God is not as distant or as unresponsive as He seems? What if scripture's promise [Romans 8:28] that "...*in all things* God works for the good of those who love Him, who have been called according to His purpose" extends to those of us who appear unable to conceive? What would that mean?

Could God possibly redeem not just the outcome of a season of infertility—as He ultimately did with Sarah—but the whole season? Could there actually be cause for hope, even a sense of blessing, in the midst of infertility?

Look at Sarah's story. In the beginning, her skepticism about conceiving a child was a grain of disbelief. But, it grew over time into a loss of expectancy, and then a loss of faith in anything outside herself. Doubt and despair darkened her thoughts, leaving no room in her heart for hope in God's promise.

Look at the trajectory of Sarah's faith as the story unfolds. She moves from initially hopeful... to skeptical... to desperate... to defeated. The more she obsesses over her doubt, worry and fear, the further she moves from peace. The closer she gets to executing her Plan B, the further she moves from God's Plan A. The more she rationalizes self-reliance, the further she moves from God-reliance.

God did not move. *Sarah did.* She chose the illusion of control over faith in the will of God. Ultimately, she trusted herself more than she trusted Him. So, she moved away from the only One with the unlimited power to realize her dream, in order to try to do it herself.

●   ●   ●

Pause and consider…. Does anything in your infertility experience compare to Sarah's trajectory? Have you been obsessing? Worrying? Fearful? Do you see how those emotions may have moved you away from God?

●   ●   ●

Why did God draw near again 13 years later? Because unlike Sarah and Abraham, He had not given up on Plan A. He reentered their story after witnessing several specific changes in them that invited Him to draw near.

First, they stopped trying to control the situation by forcing His promises on their timetable. They accepted the outcome of their ill-considered actions. They made peace with each other, the servant, and her child. And, they began to let go of their anger, resentment and fear.

Second, they settled into the silence God imposed and rediscovered stillness. After the emotional chaos of the semi-surrogacy, they re-learned how to appreciate peace and quiet.

Third, they became willing and able to listen again. At some point, they stepped outside the endless loop of infertility self-talk—and they became ready to hear someone else's voice.

●   ●   ●

They drew nearer to God, simply by no longer pulling away

●   ●   ●

Once these changes took place, they rediscovered room for God in their minds and hearts. Their drawing near to Him—*simply by no longer pulling away*—created the opportunity for Him to speak, and for them to listen. Only then did He re-deliver His message of hope, because only then was there room for Him in their story.

Has your faith life been on a trajectory like Sarah's? Has the unrelenting pressure of infertility, and its accompanying stress and grief, caused you to build a wall around your dream in order to protect it? And now, does God feel as distant and unresponsive as He did to Sarah?

If your current experience with infertility ever makes you wonder if you've been exiled from the Kingdom of God, or if at times, your broken heart prevents you from experiencing—or believing in—God's love and grace, then this message is for you: You are not lost to God. He sees your struggle, He knows your heartache, and He longs to bless the seed of hope He planted in your heart.

You are already pregnant with hope. That hope is a gift from the God who loves you and who longs to bless you beyond what you can ask or imagine [Ephesians 3:20]. That hope will carry you through the journey you've already begun.

Your trajectory doesn't have to be like Sarah's. The Bible tells us that "...faith is being sure of what we hope for and certain of what we do not see" [Hebrews 11:1]. By the end of your journey through infertility, these words will have deep meaning for you.

● ● ●

How can you find peace in the midst of uncertainty and anxiety?

● ● ●

But, in the midst of this journey, how can you be assured of what you hope for when it's not happening? How can you find peace in the midst of uncertainty and anxiety? How can you obey a God you're struggling to understand? And how can you possibly trust Him?

He has already shown, through Sarah and Abraham's story, that He is a promise-keeping God. He does not begrudge any of us the freedom to trust or mistrust Him. But, He shows us His faithfulness throughout scripture for a reason. These stories of our ancestors – our family of faith – reveal His character, His integrity, His purposefulness and His love. They demonstrate to us His consistency, His reliability, and

His trustworthiness.

Just as He did with Sarah and Abraham, God is waiting for you to let go, be still, and listen. He will speak to you through scripture, and the illumination of it by the power of the Holy Spirit.

When you listen for His voice, you will be opening your mind and heart to timeless truths. They can renew your spirit. They can nourish the seed of hope planted in your heart with sustenance only He can give.

The Bible says, "No one who trusts God like this—heart and soul—will ever regret it. It's exactly the same *no matter what a person's religious background may be*: the same God for all of us, acting the same incredibly generous way to everyone who calls out for help. Everyone who calls, 'Help, God!' gets help" [Romans 10:12, Message, italics added].

That responsive, generous God is ready to help you.

Look deeper into scripture and you will find more encouraging news. Jesus teaches, "For everyone who asks receives; he who seeks finds; and to him who knocks, the door will be opened" [Matthew 7:7-8]. Together, we can search for the God who deeply desires to be found, and we can seek His help with our infertility.

Reflections

_____
_____
_____
_____
_____
_____
_____
_____
_____
_____
_____
_____
_____
_____
_____
_____
_____
_____
_____

Sarah & Wilson

How did your story begin?

Wilson: I was 30. I was running marathons and coaching other runners with Team in Training. Sarah was one of the people I coached; that's how we met. We ran the Marine Corps Marathon together.

Sarah: We got married two years later. By the time we got married, he was 32 and I was 28. We knew we weren't ready for children. We wanted to enjoy getting to know each other and growing with each other, but we didn't want to wait forever either.

Wilson: We tried for 18 months, and it got more and more stressful. Every month the pressure built. I kept getting more frustrated, and Sarah kept getting more upset.

Sarah: Everyone says, "Don't go to the doctor until you've tried a whole year." But after trying for a while, I felt in my heart that something wasn't right. So, we kind of skipped the whole going to a regular OB and met with an infertility expert. After talking to him, we tried several things—like our IUI's.

Wilson: One of my best friends had gone through this and I was able to talk with him about what to expect. It wasn't easy on either of them. So, I was prepared that this wasn't going to be an easy thing for us. I was bracing myself that this was going to be bad.

Sarah: Meanwhile, I was looking for someone to understand what I was going through. I remember my best friend calling me and telling me she was pregnant. I was happy for her—and then I hung up and cried my eyes out.

I was searching for female friends who could understand exactly how I was feeling—girls who were in exactly the same place, not just getting pregnant the first time they tried.

Also, we were attending a couples' Sunday school class at church—which we loved—but at the time, every week someone would stand up and say, "We're expecting and we're due on this date." It was too much.

Wilson: Every time, Sarah was upset. And every time, I just wanted to yell, "Damn you!" because I knew as soon as we got in the car there'd be a breakdown, and then it would be the entire rest of the day in tears. I knew it!

Sarah: I felt very alone. I thought my faith was strong, and I was very involved in the church. But then I'd go to Sunday school, which is supposed to build you up, and it was totally breaking me down. I felt like no one around me understood how lonely I was and how sad I was.

And then teachers at school—they were always asking me, "Aren't you going to have children soon?" I mean, I love children and I'm a teacher, so what do you think? But don't ask me that! People just didn't get it. And that was so frustrating.

Wilson: But then...

Sarah: ...then, I found the women's fertility prayer group. I felt hope every time I went... but, I also felt sad whenever I left the group because I'd wonder, "How is my story going to end? What is my update next month going to be? Will I be like the girl across the circle who is still trying after 2½ years?" I kept going because I felt uplifted by prayer, but I also felt sad thinking, are the procedures ever going to work?

Meanwhile, after two failed IUI's, the doctor told me, "You need surgery." And then, after surgery, he said, "You have Stage 3 endometriosis." I had no signs for it at all. When I heard that news, I hit a wall.

What were we going to do?! IUI's weren't working….

Wilson: … and this is exactly what had happened with my friend. I was feeling like this was just the bottom of the hill, and it was going to get worse.

Sarah: I told Wilson, "I don't want to go to our Sunday school class any more. I need people I can relate to and talk with."

Wilson: So, we quit going to church.

Sarah: We needed to back away because I would get *so* upset. On Mother's Day, just sitting in church, I'd start crying. Or on baptism Sundays. I couldn't take it.

And then, there were the comments from people at church….

Wilson: …people say things so innocently…

Sarah: …like, "Wilson, you're getting older…."

Wilson: Exactly. And I'm like, this is throwing salt in the wound! You're not helping! You just get to the point where you're trying, trying, trying and nothing's happening and it becomes a robotic, monotonous thing. And after a while, you resent it. You can't work any harder and you're not achieving the goal. It's frustrating.

Sarah: That brings up a good point. My whole life, I've been blessed…

Wilson: …an overachiever….

Sarah: But really, everything we've worked for, we've gotten. We came from stable, two-parent households, both got a good education, got good jobs… everything we planned. And then came this.

I just never dreamed I would have such trouble having children. Which, of all things, God has placed me in a job with a calling to teach—which I love—and I love my kids, so why isn't God giving me kids of my own?! That's what I'd ask myself. It was so hard.

So, then you joined the infertility Bible study?

Sarah: That's when we found the class. And after the first day, I left thinking, "Oh my God, these people are like me! They understand what we're going through!"

Wilson: Yeah. At first, I didn't care about meeting anybody. I was just there to make sure that Sarah got what she needed. If she was doing okay, I could feel better. At that first class, I looked around and thought to myself, "Not one of these guys wants to be here"—and that actually made me feel better.

Sarah: Meanwhile, I left the first class with another girl's email on the back of my checkbook! I was just so desperate to reach out and talk to people who understood what I was going through.

Wilson: Then, after the first day, you could tell that everybody was going through the same thing. You didn't have to go into lots of detail and explain everything. You could tell somebody something and they'd understand it.

Sarah: We felt so close to the other couples. Right away! I felt closer to these new friends in a few weeks than to my best friend since 4th grade—because they understood what I was going through, and she couldn't understand.

Wilson: Sarah asked me a lot, "What am I doing wrong?"

Sarah: That's true. I think a lot of girls wonder about that. I knew we were on this journey for a reason, but I was getting angry that this was long enough and it was time for something to work.

I wanted to go to church and I prayed, but I didn't feel connected to God. I knew God was there, but I didn't understand why it was taking so long. I didn't get it.

Every time we went to the class, though, it helped me. It was like vitamins. You know? It gave me more energy. It made me believe, "I'm going to make my way through this." And I just felt a peace… like, it's gonna be okay.

When did things change?

Sarah: We did an IVF 5-day transfer. When we left that day, Wilson turned to me and said, "Well, the good news is that— whatever else happens—you're pregnant today."

As we drove home, I was holding my belly thinking, "I'm pregnant right now. Whatever happens…."

Wilson: So, we waited 10 days – which was an eternity….

Sarah: …and then, I did a blood test. Katherine, the nurse I'd become close to, said she'd call me at 3 pm with results. I said, "No, I'll be at school. I want to be at home." Wilson came home early so that whatever the news was, we could hug on each other.

She called and said, "You're so pregnant."

We went in for the ultrasound and the technician turned the screen around and said, "Well, it looks like you're having two." I looked at Wilson and mouthed, "Are you okay?" He just nodded. I had really wanted twins since I'm a twin, but   Wilson had said, "Let's don't get greedy—let's just pray to God for one healthy baby."

Wilson: And the babies were born at 37 weeks.

What did you learn through this infertility journey?

Sarah: I feel it strengthened our faith and brought Wilson and me closer. Meeting other couples we could relate to through the class—and especially Wilson, who'd drifted away from the church—taught us to trust in God's plan. He brought us through this storm in life and He's going to be there no matter what.

I've learned to trust that when it's out of my hands, it's still in God's control.

Wilson: Also, nobody really talks about infertility, so you feel so alone. That's part of the problem. Now, because of what we went through, people open up to me and I talk about the issues. Usually guys have an ego thing about that. I don't at all.

As a matter of fact, there's somebody in the class now who's from my office. I told my colleague, "You've got to get your wife involved." He thanked me afterwards.

I said, "You need to commit to this group. Trust me, you need a community for support."

Sarah: Most of all, we would say that if God has put this in your heart, don't give up. Don't give up. You can trust Him to do this in His time. If He gave you the hope, He will do it. So, don't give up.

Choosing to Let Go

"Let go... be still... and listen" is a more challenging prescription than any other you have ever received. Why does it feel that way? Certainly, it is much easier to say than it is to do. But, it's more than that. *Everything* about it is counterintuitive.

Letting go means unclenching the fists that are keeping a tight hold on the dream of becoming parents. That is not easy. It means relinquishing control. Or worse, it means acknowledging that control is, and always has been, an illusion—an extremely comforting, reassuring one.

Now, if you choose to let go, the dream may suddenly feel at risk in a new way. Who will protect it if you let go? Infertility seems so capricious. Letting go evokes anxious feelings of surrender that beckon hopelessness, loss, and defeat.

Despite these feelings of vulnerability, you will need to release your grasp and open your fists if you want God's best. He won't give what you aren't ready and willing to receive. He will not force the plans He has for you into your life. He will not insist on His way.

He has given you the freedom to choose the illusion of control over trust in Him. But He longs to bring the blessing of the realized dream into your life. He is waiting for you to choose—His plan, or your own. By choosing to trust Him enough to lay open your hands, you signal: I willingly accept whatever You intend to give me.

Being still and listening—the rest of the prescription—
go hand-in-hand. It is impossible to hear, much less listen to and
absorb, things that are said to you when you are frantically busy.
Especially if that busyness is overlaid with constant, worried
self-talk: "What if I can't...?" "What if we don't...?" "What if
this doesn't...?"

In order to take God's words deep into your heart, in
order to allow them to alter your thoughts and ease your mind,
you will need to calm yourself. To set aside racing thoughts and
growing fears. You will need to find a way to be still, to create
the possibility of a peaceful receptiveness that enables Him to
speak and be heard.

◉　◉　◉

Pause and consider.... Do you trust God enough to let go, be
still, and listen? Are you wondering, why even try?

◉　◉　◉

How? How is it possible?! And if you aren't sure you
trust God completely, why would you even try?

The easy question to answer is, "Why even try?" There
are negative reasons: because you are out of options, because
nothing else works, because you have reached your limits and
can't push past them.

There are also positive reasons. Mainly, because if the
only communication between you and God is an urgent 911, you
are missing out on the blessings that come with
hearing Him speak to you regularly. Blessings
like peace, patience, comfort, trust, confidence,
assurance—and the renewal of God-given hope.

Is it even possible to listen to God? Who
actually hears God talking these days? It would
be wonderful to have dreams or visions. Or better
yet, what about real-time appearances by God—

◉　◉　◉

How *can* you
hear God
speak to you?

◉　◉　◉

like Abraham experienced? Overhearing God telling His plans for you to someone else—like Sarah did—would definitely help. But, most likely, that hasn't happened to you yet. And truthfully, you don't expect it to. So, how *can* you hear God speak to you?

In our group, we start by bathing our minds and hearts in promises God makes to us through scripture.

What does that mean? Sometimes the word "marinate" helps couples understand our objective. We want to spend time soaking in and soaking up the truths of the Bible that speak directly to our current circumstance. In so doing, we allow ourselves to be transformed in a way that adds a depth, meaning and new flavor to our experience.

First, we read aloud, giving the words on the page time to seep into our spirits as we read them slowly and mindfully together. Then, we dig deep beneath the surface of the words to the life-giving truths that underlie them.

As we do, certain insights will suddenly spark someone in the group. They will see with new clarity something they had not seen before. As they share their realizations, other people will resonate in response—or experience their own sudden epiphany. These moments of deeply personalized understanding are often accompanied by a sudden sense of relief, and followed by a wave of peace. This is the Holy Spirit enabling us to receive the personalized word of God.

This is how God begins to speak hope to infertile faith.

Whenever we start a new infertility group, we begin looking in a particular Bible verse for the God of Abraham and Sarah, the one who cares about the struggles of infertile couples.

Take the time to read it over slowly, and then consider all that this promise may mean for you:

"For I know the plans I have for you," declares the Lord; "plans to prosper you and not to harm you, plans to give you hope and a future."   *- Jeremiah 29:11*

• • •

Pause and consider.... Does this verse satisfyingly address the feeling that God is unresponsive and unmoved? Do your head and heart agree on that? If you re-read the verse, do you find any cause for hope? If so, what is it?

• • •

Sometimes, hearing God's voice depends on knowing how to listen for it.

Let's begin with the phrase, "For I know the plans...." God is saying that His plans are preconceived and intentional. They precede this moment in time, and they are not random or arbitrary. They are neither last-minute nor a whim. These are plans designed specifically for you, based on His knowledge of all things and His intention to bless you.

"... plans I have for you...." *I* have for you. *I* have. Not plans I know *you* have for you, or plans I know you *want* Me to have for you. These plans are God's best for you. Because of your freedom to make choices of all kinds (free will), you may never see these plans come to fruition if you choose your plans over God's. Sarah chose not to wait... not to believe... not to trust any plan but her own. But note, even that did not ultimately thwart God's plan for her.

> God has blessings planned for you; He wants to give you His very best

"...declares the Lord;..." God is announcing these plans to you with conviction. He is positive of their existence prior to their execution. The statement, "I know the plans I have for you" carries the full weight and authority of the King who declares them. It is so. He is certain.

"...Plans to prosper you...." The use of active voice reinforces that God will be taking action for your benefit. He intends to prosper you, or to set in motion the prosperity that He wills for you. You will receive the action, receive the blessing that is His gift to you.

"...and not to harm you...." God is making two overlapping promises. He plans to prosper you *and* not to harm you. Like a Venn diagram, this area of overlap indicates your maximum benefit. He intends to help you, *and* not to hurt you. He intends to lift you up, *and* not to hold you back. He plans to bless you, *and* not to curse you. He is for you, *and* not against you.

Note, though, that this portion of His promise is not a talisman against harm. Sarah exercised her free will, setting off a chain reaction that caused harm to her marriage, her relationship with her servant, her faith, and her emotional well-being.

You, too, are free to make choices that cause harm. But, God does not plan to harm you. In fact, the Bible reassures us that "...God causes everything to work together *for the good* of those who love God and are called according to His purpose for them" [Romans 8:28, NLT].

Remember?

"...plans to give you hope...." The use of active voice and the verb "give" reminds again that God will be taking the action; you will be on the receiving end. He will give you hope that originates with Him. Because He is a promise-keeping God, that hope will have a different kind of staying power than the self-based hope you prop up with busyness and frantic efforts to control. It will be vital and full of life. It will be sustained by *His* will, not just your own.

> Do you hear God's voice of reassurance? You can trust His plan for you

"...and a future...." Again, God makes two overlapping promises. He will give you hope *and* give you a future. Not just one or the other, but both. One gift for the waiting time (hope), and another gift of pending blessings (a future). One you need now; one you can await with anticipation and gratitude. The knowledge that you have both can bring you peace—now, and always.

Taken as a whole message, these verses make clear that God is proactively planning abundant blessings for you! Do you hear His voice of reassurance? He is saying, "You can relinquish control and trust Me. You can let go." Your response should be to anticipate these blessings confidently and thrive in the meantime.

But it's not that easy.

Why not? Why is it so hard to let go?

The problem is: "For I know..." God has made plans that God-only knows. The excruciating challenge is, *you* don't know. And you won't know until after-the-fact. If you are going to relinquish control to God, you will have to do so without knowing His plans. You will have to trust Him in the midst of uncertainty.

Can you trust God to keep promises in your life—just as He does in scripture?

⬤   ⬤   ⬤

Pause and consider.... What do you believe about God's trustworthiness? Why do you feel the way you do? Have other people's experiences affected your ability to trust God? How so?

⬤   ⬤   ⬤

Trust God in the midst of uncertainty....

Did you feel that sudden drop in the pit of your stomach, as if the emotional roller coaster just went into a freefall? That is the feeling many couples have when they face the prospect of handing their dream over to God. Like you, they've come face-to-face with the realization that they don't trust Him as much as they thought they did, or wish they could.

Infertility shows you the limits of your faith in a way that is inescapable. You discover that letting go completely feels impossible because you don't trust God—not enough to give

Him control. At the same time, infertility reveals the limits of your own power. You can't force the outcome you want on your timetable, no matter how much you spend or how hard you try.

Like Sarah, you could force *something* (or try to), but God's best is out of reach without Him. You're stuck, seemingly with no way forward.

When confronted with these limits, couples struggle mightily to find a way through the impasse. They come to our group longing to be still... and listen... because the more they hear about abundant blessings, the better they feel. At least, temporarily.

They are eager to bask in the promises of God's goodness, and readily commit to coming weekly to hear more about the purpose of His plans for them. That good news is like light at the end of the tunnel, leading them to the peace and (hopefully) the baby they long for. But letting go is another story.

Now comes a difficult choice...

At some point, the lack of forward progress becomes unbearable. Couples face a choice. They can sacrifice their dream... or their faith in a loving, responsive God... or their (illusion of) control. It's a *very* difficult choice.

The first option is to let the dream of a baby die. Sometimes, relationships implode under the constant pressure of infertility. After an agonizing struggle, the dream dies and the relationship dies with it. The only choice left is whether to begin trying again with someone new, or seek out a partner who doesn't want children.

Sometimes, *before* the relationship implodes, one person concludes that the dream must die or the relationship will. So, a triage decision must be made. In order to protect their future as a couple, these spouses choose to grieve the death of the parenthood dream, and move on together—childless.

The second option is to keep the dream alive, but let faith in God's faithfulness die. Couples sometimes recoil when this option is voiced to them. But in truth, it only speaks what has already been happening. Faith has been withering... shriveling to a small speck in the face of their infertility experience.

Couples who choose this path believe there is no real choice. Their infertile faith cannot find sufficient hope in God's promises, or sufficient evidence in their experience thus far, to trust Him. Instead, they elect to trust the worldly success formula that equates results with effort, and good outcomes with control.

Some couples who make this choice reason that if God cared as much as they do about the dream, it would happen. He would make it happen. The fact that it hasn't happened is clearly evidence He doesn't care. So, He can't be put in charge. It's too risky. Too dangerous.

> Some couples believe putting God in charge is too risky

Other couples openly admit they would be willing to entrust their dream to God if He would just facilitate trust by sharing the details of the plan. When will it happen? And how?

I've heard couples say, "If we knew the details, we could relax. We could live our lives in peace, and stop putting everything else on hold while we wait for a baby." These couples are willing to give up control *if* God will give up the details of His plan.

Do you see the problem? These couples want to shrink God to a size they can manage—limiting His actions to the ones they know to anticipate. They want God's power at work in their lives, but under their supervision and with their buy-in. That's not letting go. It's just a different way of maintaining control.

When God doesn't provide the information these couples want, they conclude the deal is off. Negotiations are over. And then, whether in anger or despair, they rationalize they have no choice but to maintain a tight grip on the situation. They have made an unconscious decision to turn their back on God— just to maintain the illusion of control.

• • •

Pause and consider.... Has either of these options—letting the dream die, or no longer trusting God—occurred to you? What does your head tell you about what to choose? What about your heart? Does your spouse share your feelings?

• • •

The third option is to let the illusion of control "die," and to entrust the dream to God, the dream-giver. This is the ultimate letting go. It is willful denial of self, combined with intentional faith in God's faithfulness. It is unclenching the fists that have clung to the dream and turning our palms upward in faithful supplication.

It takes a tremendous act of courage because it seems so counterintuitive. It requires saying "no" to Sarah's path, and "yes" to humility and patience. It means dying to the part of us that wants to push, to control, to have our way—*now!* And instead, choosing to wait for God's best, in His timing.

• • •

We *can* experience peace in the midst of uncertainty

• • •

If we can believe that God the promise-maker is also a promise-keeper, we will be able to envision choosing this third way forward. We will be able to imagine choosing to trust God, in spite of infertility's (seeming) evidence to the contrary.

We will be able to see ourselves claiming the promise that He is already at work transforming His best plans into reality. And, we will be able to find peace in the midst of uncertainty.

Does anyone longing for a baby ever feel able to make this choice? *Do you*? The only way to answer this question is to ask the deeper question: Can God be trusted?

The answer is… Yes.

But how?

It is possible in response to a gift God gives all of us. That gift is the paradoxical gift of withholding. God intentionally gives us *less* information about our future as parents than He ultimately gave Abraham and Sarah, so that we will need to exert more faith, to stretch in the direction of believing—despite not seeing—that He is already at work. To reach for Him, long for Him, search for Him... that is the gift to us: the awakening of an urgent desire to find Him, draw near to Him, and deepen our trust in Him.

God does not expect blind faith from us. Abraham and Sarah's story enables us to see first-hand how God works in the life of an infertile couple. The story lets us peek behind the scenes.

It pulls back the veil to allow us to see God's plan-making intentionality before-the-fact (making His initial promise to Abraham 25 years before Isaac was born). And then, to see His faithfulness in "real time," as the story unfolds through the book of Genesis.

> We can see
> first-hand
> how God works
> in the life
> of an
> infertile couple

All together, this allows us to see how God's plans are born into the natural world, as they transition from sacred promise to long-awaited reality.

Sarah and Abraham's story also enables us to see the truth of the verse we considered earlier, Jeremiah 29:11. God reveals—to them, and to us—that He does have plans to prosper and not to harm those He loves. They are plans for hope and a future. And those plans are realized in His perfect timing, according to His will and by His power.

He demonstrates His abundant goodness by giving Sarah and Abraham what they long for—in a miraculous way that makes it unmistakably clear it's His doing. His blessing. His perfect plan.

Ultimately, the story is an invitation to accept on faith that the God of Abraham and Sarah is also our God. That His desire to bless our dream is as strong as His determination to bless them and theirs. And, that His faithfulness endures to all generations [Psalm 100:5].

●　　●　　●

Pause and consider.... Do you believe God can truly redeem a season of infertility? If so, do you want the God of Sarah and Abraham to be part of your infertility story? Has this lesson given you any real cause for hope that He already is—or that He can be?

●　　●　　●

Every infertile couple that comes to our group wants to trust God. The Bible verse of promise for hope and a future—along with the incredible miracle of Isaac's conception and birth—inspires couples to reexamine their faith in light of the choice they must make about how to move forward. Some start questioning and searching for God with a new urgency. They begin to dig much deeper.

> *If God can be trusted, then that could change everything about infertility*

If God can be trusted, they reason, then the choice to let go of (the illusion of) control—and all the struggling and stress that accompanies it—will be the one to make. The best, and maybe only, way through the impasse... to the dream. To the future they want. And to peace.

If God can be trusted, they realize, then letting go could very well open doors that would not otherwise be opened. It could create opportunities that might otherwise never exist. It could unleash previously unimagined possibilities. And in the cascading river of possibilities, there could be—would be—one perfect option: God's very best.

So, can He be trusted? Every couple will need to answer this question for themselves. To do so, they will have to bypass the other major stumbling block to trust. They must confront the painful question they've tried so hard to avoid: "Why, God?"

Reflections

Angela & Sean

How did your story begin?

Angela: We were both 25 when we got married. I wanted to enjoy the marriage. I didn't want to throw a kid in there and then try to find out who my husband was. I wanted them one at a time.

Sean: We both wanted kids. I wanted them sooner than she did, but we decided to wait because we weren't financially ready.

Angela: Or mature!

Sean: We decided to wait and get our careers on track, get some traveling out of the way…. It was all about us—and then, we'd get to the kid thing.

Angela: We didn't realize we had a problem until I thought I was having appendicitis. I went to the ER and it turned out I had an ectopic pregnancy.

We thought—like everyone else—that you get off birth control, wait six months and "boom" you get pregnant. But first I had the ectopic pregnancy, then a cyst, then surgery for a closed tube, and then a miscarriage…. We realized we needed help.

Sean: My first thought was, "Crap, we were on birth control for ten years. That's the problem."

Angela: My mom would send me these articles that were in the paper about how birth control affects fertility. We always wondered if that was the problem—if we had waited too long.

But, maybe we weren't letting God work in His way, and that was why we had infertility. Maybe we didn't let this happen naturally, so this was my punishment.

Sean: Anyway… we did basal temperature and ovulation kits.

Angela: We started Clomid for 6 months. That didn't work. We started with IUI. It was just the two of us going through it. No support group. No friends going through it.

Sean: I didn't tell my parents.

Angela: We had *no* support network, and we weren't telling anyone what was happening.

Sean: Then, we moved and we had to find a new doctor and get all the tests done again. To make it more difficult, the doctor we had been going to was one of the top in the nation in infertility. We were so disappointed…

Angela: …if he couldn't be successful, what were the odds that someone else could be?

Sean: There was definitely stress with that. Should we be doing this? Or should we move back? So much stress.

We'd had a church… but when we moved, we were so engulfed with all of this that we stopped going regularly.

Angela: At that point, we'd already had two failed IUI's and two miscarriages. We went to church on Mother's Day weekend and I had a really hard time. I couldn't make it through the service, so we got up to leave.

But, I saw in the bulletin that there was going to be a

class for infertile couples. I showed it to Sean and said, "Let's try this." Until then, I thought it was just me.

Sean: I knew this was something that would let her get things out. She was having breakdowns where she'd go in our room to cry. She was pulling away and trying to hide it from me.

Angela: He put the class on his calendar so we'd be sure to go!

Sean: I was going to support her. She needed something. I didn't necessarily think it was going to fix anything. But I thought it was going to be a place where she could make connections with other people.

How did coming to the class help you?

Angela: By the time the class started, we'd had a failed IVF, gone through shots…. I was emotionally and spiritually a wreck. I still believed in God and the church, but I wondered, "Why? What did I do wrong? Something before our marriage? During our marriage?" Why was this happening to me?

Sean: We hadn't brought the question of "why?" to God yet. I believed in God, but I wasn't praying. I wasn't reading the Bible. We would go to church and go through the motions, but I wasn't getting any traction.

Maybe the reason our timeline was pushed out was that we had to be in a situation that would make us grow. The way we had to grow was to ask these questions.

Angela: It was the perfect time for the class to start.

Sean: I did have a few questions. Were there going to be guys there? Was I going to be in a roomful of women and they were all going to be crying? The only expectation I had was that it would be good for Angela.

Angela: [laughing] He hoped I'd stop crying.

Sean: It turned out to be great, though. We needed to build a community and see other people going through infertility.

Angela: We went through the whole 10-week class. Two or three people out of the group were successful during that time; they got pregnant. On the one hand, I was thinking—Oh good, this can work. Maybe they're getting rewarded for how faithful they've been. But there was also the other side of me thinking— Why her and not me? Why doesn't God think I should conceive?

I did take that question to God, but I had to do it twice.

The first time was after the class had ended. I was still going to the fertility prayer group—which was my saving grace when the class wasn't there—and I met a girl who had been through numerous failed IVF's. Many more than I had. One day, she announced she was pregnant with twins.

I said, "What'd you do? How did it work?" I wanted to know what the answer was.

She said, "I gave it to God."

I remember thinking—Oh come on, what an expected answer. So, I was like, "Really, how'd you do it?"

And she said, "I just gave it to God."

In my mind I'm thinking—Great, I should've known I would hear this. I felt very skeptical, thinking, Oh sure, that's all it takes.

Later that night, I was upstairs and I prayed and said, "Okay, God, this is in your hands." I thought I'd try it. Nothing happened the next month. We had another failed IVF. I remember thinking—Well, giving it to God didn't work. So then, I was truly at my wits' end.

Then one night, I had been to another prayer meeting that was very emotional. I couldn't share my story without bawling. I was just a wreck. I remember coming home and that night I gave it to God again. But this time, I gave it *all*—heart and soul.

It wasn't rehearsed; it was totally spontaneous. It was, "I'm done. I can't handle another cycle. I can't handle another miscarriage. I can't handle the roller coaster ride every month. I give up. I quit. It's yours. It's all yours."

Sean: The next week, we found out that we had reached the end of the road. There wasn't much more we could try. The doctors said, "We think she has an autoimmune deficiency. We're going to put her on some medicine and see if that helps...."

Angela: ...but they were at the end of the tests they could do.

Sean: They said, "We'll start her on XYZ vitamins." The next month, we went in for a blood test as we were getting ready to do another IVF transfer... and we found out she was pregnant.

They told us and it was like, "No. *Is that a joke*?!" We asked if it could have been the vitamins, but they said, No—her body hadn't had time to respond to them yet.

Truthfully, I don't think it was medical. I think this was divine intervention. I attribute the pregnancy to her giving it up to God. When they told us there was no medical explanation for her getting pregnant...

Angela: ... they truly couldn't explain it...

Sean: ...that meant to us that there was something beyond what people could control. That helped me see God in it.

Angela: I agree, it was the letting go. It was truly and respectfully giving it to God and saying, "I'm done. I give it to your hands." After I did that, I didn't take temperatures or watch the calendar or do anything. For me, that was the turning point. Totally letting go—that's what changed things.

Sean: After that point, everything started going right. Everything started blossoming. Like relationships... we were part of a community. We had connections. We felt like we knew what other people in the class were going through and we could talk about it. A whole world opened. Everything funneled into this one point... and then everything blossomed out of it.

Angela: After baby #1, we didn't know if we'd ever have another one. We decided to do another frozen cycle... but then, we found out I was pregnant again! I was eight weeks along.

When they told me, I thought "This can't be right. My body doesn't work. I've been told by doctors that I'll have a hard time. Why would this happen now?" But this time, I think we were spiritually ready.

Sean: The crazy thing is, at that time, there was a whole whirlwind outside our lives. Angela's father had terminal cancer. Her sister had terminal cancer. We were sure we couldn't have another child.

Then, Angela's dad passed. Then, she lost her job. Then, we were driving back-and-forth to see her sister all the time.... and then, we got pregnant.

What did you learn from this experience?

Angela: I think, through this journey, I learned that there's a reason for everything. I may not like it, I may not be happy about it, and I don't always know why, but I can still find peace. I can let go. And that's different for me.

Sean: I'd say the blessing is that, without this trial, I don't know that I'd have a relationship with Jesus Christ. I don't think he was on my radar. But there's definitely a connection now! That's a huge change for me.

Angela: Yeah. Before, God was in the backseat, but He was in the car. Now, if He's not driving, at least He's in the front seat with me. I may not walk around quoting scripture, but I feel confident that even if I'm scared, the way He wants things is how it will work out—if I trust Him.

Sean: Our faith is getting stronger. It's not just habit or ritual any more. Our prayers are personal. There is a relationship behind those prayers now.

Asking "Why?"

There is something comforting about trusting that a bad day doesn't come looking for you. You stumble across it or tumble into it, but it doesn't hold meaning any deeper than "watch out next time."

You can console yourself with reassurances: it could happen to anyone—it's just bad luck. Of course, it didn't happen to just anyone. It happened to you. But, by trying harder or staying more alert, you tell yourself, you can surely avert a similar disaster tomorrow. You pull yourself up by the bootstraps, determined to change your luck. And soon enough, you usually do.

In a season of infertility, such empty reassurances feel like whistling in the dark. This is a different kind of bad. It's a string of bad days that drags on and on and on. It settles into both life and spirit with an unnerving sense of permanence. The search for meaning in this experience goes much deeper—to a quest for reasons, a longing for understanding, and a hunger for comfort that reaches the soul.

The misery brings with it a profound sense of isolation. You may have twelve million companions in this experience, but they are nowhere to be found. Rarely do they choose to self-identify; the social stigma is too powerful. So, even as your spirit craves companionship, you feel increasingly apart, chosen for suffering you do not understand. Separated from everything "normal," you seem to be drifting further and further away from anything familiar. Where to? And why is God allowing this to happen?

When life is unfolding according to plan, most of us prefer to side-step the broad philosophical question of why people suffer, as if suffering itself could be contagious. But infertility propels the question to the forefront with desperate urgency. The question becomes much more personal—"why *me*?"—and insistent when the suffering is our own.

In the beginning, all thoughts and feelings about infertility spring from the big, central question: "WHY?" With time, and without conceiving, the "why?" multiplies and metastasizes. Its offshoots begin to spring up everywhere. Why us? Why me? Why now? Why not? Why them?

> *Why* is God allowing this to happen?

Anxiety feeds the questions. Doubt does, too. Jealousy poisons many thoughts with toxic envy. The "why?" spreads to cover all aspects of the struggle to get pregnant, sinking its roots deep into the spirit: Why does everyone else...? Why haven't we...? Why did they...? Why, if we...? Why, if they...? Why not us?!

＊　＊　＊

Pause and consider.... Have you been wondering if God is ignoring your pleas, refusing to answer "why?" What have you told yourself about His apparent silence?

＊　＊　＊

In the absence of clear answers, partners sometimes turn on one another: Why don't you...?! Why aren't you...?! Why can't you...?! As if the one soul they've counted on for success has intentionally caused this problem. The cycle of blame-denial-confusion takes hold and emotional turbulence becomes the norm. Anger pitches a tent—as does its alter ego, depression (which is just anger turned inward).

The tenor of the question changes as stress levels escalate, but the content rarely does. Throughout this crazy, accelerating rollercoaster ride, the question remains: "Why?!"

It is our nature as human beings to crave control. Having been created with freedom of choice, we long to exercise it: *I choose to start a family now*. When we can't, we turn to science for explanations and solutions. Frequently, though, there are no clear answers.

It could be you. It might be me. It doesn't look like anything is wrong, but clearly something isn't right. Even when the factual reasons become clear, something deep inside us still needs to ask, "Why?"

If we look cautiously behind that question, we often find Fear hiding in the shadows. It is a deep and visceral fear that putting "why?" questions to God is a dangerous idea. We may get answers we don't like, or can't handle. What if we tempt Fate, or incite wrath? We may learn the truth and no longer be able to deny it.

> • • •
>
> We fear that asking God "why?" may be dangerous
>
> • • •

Some of us wonder if the truth may be premised on cause and effect. Most of life seems to work that way. So, if infertility is the effect, what—or who—is the cause? That's a scary question. The thought of actually opening this Pandora's box is unnerving. Could infertility be a punishment for something? Is that how God works? Does He intentionally withhold blessings, as well as give them? Is He doing that now?

Rather than risk hearing the worst possible answers, we unconsciously disconnect from God. We shut down communications. Rather than confront Him with our deepest, most heartbreaking questions, we hide our hearts and deny these fears even to ourselves. We're too vulnerable already.

We may go through the motions of prayer, but we don't

hear God…, and we certainly don't feel heard. And then, we wonder where God is. Why has He abandoned us when we need Him most? *The truth is, God hasn't abandoned us. We are the ones who have pulled away.*

When we refuse to bring the question "why?' to the only One who can answer, our question surfaces in disguise—cloaked in depression or fury. We break down crying, begging to know why, but stay too absorbed in self-pity to hear God answer. Or, we risk ranting **"why?!"**, but stay too angry at Him to listen for a response. We consume tremendous emotional energy holding off the only One who can truly understand and answer us.

Why?

It may be that God brings us to this struggle, this head-on collision between the reality of childlessness and the limits of our faith, to show us that we don't actually trust Him. Not His love or His motives.

Maybe we don't believe that He hears us and cares—at least, not about this. Maybe we don't feel safe in our relationship with Him, and so we don't dare risk confronting Him for fear that bad will get worse. Maybe we feel lost to Him, or forgotten. Maybe we feel punished and angry. Maybe we are afraid. Maybe all these things. Maybe more.

> Our struggle reveals the limits of our trust in God, and in His motives

This much we know: we can't hear His answer to the question our souls cry out, and our loneliness and suffering continue. We need God the promise-keeper to break through to us, to seek and find us in this dark place and lead us into the light. This is the prayer of the brokenhearted which brings us to the Bible, looking for answers and listening for God's voice.

Throughout the Bible, we find stories of believers who struggle with the same questions infertile couples face. Why must we suffer? Why does God allow it? Does God see it? Does He care? When we explore these Bible stories in our group, we find profoundly relevant messages that speak directly into hearts longing for answers.

We begin with the story of Job.

From his perspective, Job's experience is one of prolonged suffering without apparent cause. Job is a good, faithful man who suddenly finds himself suffering the loss of his home, his wealth, his material possessions, his children, his health…. The seeming randomness of this nightmare only compounds his grief.

For much of the story, he clings to his faith despite his wife's advice to curse God and die, and his friends' consensus that somehow Job has brought this on himself.

For 38 chapters, Job wrestles with the question "why?" and the total silence of God. Where is He? Hasn't Job been faithful and good? Hasn't he walked the path of the righteous? Finally, he can take no more. His words lay bare his anguish, "I cry out to you, O God, but you do not answer; I stand up, but you merely look at me. You turn on me ruthlessly; with the might of your hand you attack me" [Job30:20-21].

There it is… the truth in Job's heart: God is doing this, and He doesn't care that it's killing me.

Job's honesty shocks the couples who have never heard his story. They may have heard of the "patience of Job," but not the agony or the fury.

●   ●   ●

Pause and consider…. Does Job's story resonate with you? How so? When you hear his outburst, how do you feel? What thoughts or feelings is he expressing that you share? How safe do you feel revealing those? Why?

●   ●   ●

Job's story is suddenly compelling in a new way. It is not just a story of unending suffering. His agonized cry draws us in because this is a man who understands devastating tragedies—and all the emotions that accompany them. He knows what it's like to be abandoned by God, and he's not afraid to say so.

When I ask infertile couples if Job's experience feels familiar to them, responses range from stunned silence, to bitter laughter, to tears. This *is* the experience of infertility: compounding losses, escalating grief, a growing sense of helplessness, emotional abandonment by a spouse, useless advice from friends, the deeply wounding question, "Do you think God is punishing you for something?," and anger born out of seemingly pointless pain and ongoing suffering.

Yes, this feels familiar! So does the sense that this experience threatens to destroy whatever relationship may have existed with God prior to all of this.

Having bonded rapidly with their new brother in the fraternity of grief, couples are eager to hear the end of his story. Does he renounce God? Die suddenly? What happens—and why?

The answer is that two encounters—one with a friend, and one with God—enable Job to realize that his limited understanding of God's plans and purpose brought on his doubt and despair. The circumstances themselves have not destroyed Job's faith; it is the growing, obsessive focus on his own perspective (rather than God's) that blinds Job to the truth of God's goodness, rapidly undermining his trust and crippling his faith.

⚫   ⚫   ⚫

Pause and consider.... Does "obsessive focus" describe your perspective on infertility? Might that be undermining your trust? Crippling your faith? Blinding you to God's presence?

⚫   ⚫   ⚫

Job is humbled by the realization that God has not failed him or abandoned him. He voices his remorse to God: "I know that you can do all things; no plan of yours can be thwarted. Surely I spoke of things I did not understand, things too wonderful for me to know" [Job 42:2-3]. What is God's response? The Bible says God heaps blessings on Job, giving him twice as much of everything as he had before his suffering began [Job 42:10-12].

So, how does Job's story help infertile couples? What about it is relevant to the struggle with infertility?

Several things.

First, Job's epiphany: focusing on his own perspective blinded him to the Truth, undermined his trust and crippled his faith. Seeing this clearly radically alters Job's experience of his circumstances. His thoughts and feelings—and ultimately, his circumstances—change when his attitude of entitled bitterness becomes one of humble gratitude.

● ● ●

Job's insight raises the possibility of us shifting perspective

● ● ●

Job's insight raises the possibility of us shifting our perspective—from one which blinds us to the Truth, undermines our trust and cripples our faith, to one which has the opposite effect—one which opens our eyes to the Truth, strengthens our trust and energizes our faith. This *is* possible.

To do it, we must learn to see our experience from God's perspective, with faith in the promise that "all things work together for good…", and trust in God's plan "to prosper you and not to harm you, to give you hope and a future"… *even when our circumstances suggest otherwise.*

Like Job, we need to realize that the world's equation— seeing is believing— is a self-absorbed, show-me perspective. It makes faith contingent on continuous, tangible evidence of God's favor. So, when blessings cease to flow (or seem to), this kind of faith crumples to the ground and despair takes over.

This kind of faith may incorporate belief in God's existence, but it does not trust His faithfulness, His plan or His timing. Like Job, we must rediscover the truth that God is always faithful; only our trust in His faithfulness is sporadic.

Why does consistently trusting God seem so monumentally difficult? Because we are unable to see beyond **I WANT** and **NOW**. We are consumed with thoughts of what we do not have, and how long we must wait to have it. We experience suffering as never-ending and all-encompassing, and God as distant and dispassionate.

● ● ●

We are often unable to see beyond I WANT and NOW

● ● ●

Meanwhile, we take for granted the many blessings that arrive daily, with very little fanfare. And, we don't recognize many more that present themselves as blessings-in-disguise.

We are constantly filled with thoughts of ourselves. Too often, this translates into trusting only ourselves and our own perceptions.

Like Job, we need to turn away from the world's seeing-is-believing mindset, and instead, learn to believe even when we cannot see—that we can trust God is at work, that He knows our needs, that He has a perfect plan, and that He is acting through our circumstances to accomplish His will in His perfect timing.

How can we do that?

How did Job do that? By immersing himself—not in thoughts of his own suffering, but in thoughts of who God is and all He has done. That immersion led Job to the humble realization that God's thoughts were beyond his ability to comprehend. Acknowledging that limitation, Job chose to trust God *by faith* [Job 42:2-3].

In the Bible, God says," My thoughts are not your thoughts, neither are your ways my ways. As the heavens are higher than the earth, so are my ways higher than your ways and my thoughts than your thoughts" [Isaiah 55:8-9].

If we can embrace a Job-like shift in our perspective—from a me-centric view of our experience, to a God-centered one—it will bring us the peace we need, even in the absence of the information we want.

How? By shifting the source of our peace from what we see to whom we trust: the unchanging God of the universe. Our peace will not rely on our own understanding, vision or circumstances. Instead, it will be rooted in the eternal truth of who God is and what our relationship with Him is intended to be: you will be My people, and I will be your God [Exodus 6:7].

That is the essence of Job's epiphany.

●　●　●

Pause and consider.... Can you envision shifting the source of your peace from what-you-see to whom-you-trust? What is preventing you from choosing to make that shift: Fear? Doubt? Anger? The need for control? What do you gain by clinging to a perspective that brings you no peace? Is that choice worth reconsidering?

●　●　●

Job's epiphany sounds compelling, and it obviously enabled Job to withstand countless tragedies with his faith intact. But is it really possible for *us* to make such a dramatic shift in perspective?

This is the second way in which Job's story speaks meaningfully to infertile couples. We stand outside Job's story, so we can view it with more objectivity than our own.

When Job demands to know, "why God?!" we understand his bitterness and the feeling that his suffering is pointless. In a sense, we see ourselves in him. But at the same time, we know the back story and can view Job from God's perspective, knowing—as God does—that this suffering is the result of a bet with Satan, that it will be temporary, and that abundant blessings await at the end of the story.

When we see clearly the differences between these two

perspectives, we want to step into the story and point out to Job: (1) it's not just about you, (2) sometimes perception is not reality, and (3) there is a larger story.

If only he could recognize these truths without having to suffer for 38 chapters! He would stop misinterpreting God's motives and misunderstanding His apparent absence. He would find peace so much sooner.

We cannot step in to enlighten Job... *but*, we can apply these insights to our own story. If and when we do, we will discover that it helps us make the shift from our limited perspective to God's "all things work together for good" perspective.

> We can apply Job's learning to our own story

Let's start at the beginning of our own infertility stories. Truth be told, we assume that if we are suffering, then it *is* about us, our perceptions *are* reality, and we *are* the central characters in the story that matters most.

Spoken aloud, that sounds arrogantly self-important. But, it's the truth of the human perspective—each of us thinks: It's all about me. We place ourselves and these assumptions at the center of the question when we ask, "Why, God? Why am I suffering? Why don't you care?"

Job's story reminds us that it's not always about us. Job's story is also about spiritual warfare, tests of faith, different perspectives on the same circumstances (voiced alternately by Job, his wife, his friends, and God), and the character of God. So might ours be.

* * *

Pause and consider.... Could your infertility story possibly be about anything besides you? If so, what might that be? How does acknowledging this possibility change the way you see your experience?

* * *

Job's story reminds us that perceptions are not always reality. Job's feelings of despair, grief and betrayal are not evidence of God's heartlessness. Job's thoughts about God's willful infliction of pain are not proof such a thing has occurred.

●　●　●

Pause and consider.... Might this be the case in your story, too? Might your thoughts and feelings about God's role in your experience be as misguided as Job's?

●　●　●

Job's story also reminds us that there is a larger story—sometimes several—in which we unknowingly play a small, but often critical, role. Job is part of the larger story of spiritual warfare, and the even larger story of God's ever-fickle faithful and His desire to mature their fearful uncertainty into a more substantial faith.

The largest story of all is Job's role in the world's best-read book, the Bible, which has survived for millennia and spoken to billions of people worldwide about suffering, faith and redemption. Odds are, we are part of a larger story, too. Our limited ability to understand does not make it any less real, or any less vital to the Kingdom.

●　●　●

Pause and consider.... Taken together, do the three truths of Job's story—it's not just about you; sometimes perception is not reality; and, there is a larger story—begin to alter your perspective on your infertility experience? How so?

●　●　●

These ideas cause most couples to respond first with relief. They see that most of their worst fears are imagined. They aren't actually being punished, humiliated, condemned, or ignored. God isn't arbitrarily withholding their heart's desire. As with Job, their story is probably about other things entirely.

Self-conscious amusement follows soon after. The truth of all three statements—it's not always about you; sometimes perception is not reality; there is a larger story—is intuitively obvious. *Of course, it's not always about me. Yes, sometimes my perceptions have nothing to do with reality. And often, there is a larger story... and I'm just a small part of it.*

Couples can humbly acknowledge their self-absorption and, for the first time, begin to understand how it has interfered with seeing their circumstances from God's perspective.

When we admit to ourselves our tendency to view life as revolving around us, we open the door to a new way of seeing. Now, we are ready to search out God's vision for our lives. Can we learn to see from His perspective?

> Humility can open the door to a new way of seeing our circumstances

In the Bible, God says, "See, I am doing a new thing! Now it springs up; do you not perceive it?" [Isaiah 43:19]. So far, we have not. Will we? Can we?

Questions of perspective and our ability to trust God's motives fill our thoughts as, together, we set off on a spiritual journey that will be life-changing.

●　●　●

Pause and consider.... At this point, can you imagine shifting your perspective to one more like God's? What might that shift cost you? How might you benefit? Do you believe it is worth whatever risk you perceive?

●　●　●

Reflections

Amy & Trey

How did your story begin?

Trey: We got married in 2001. When we started thinking about having kids—and it's kind of funny to look back on it now—I said, "I don't want a December baby, and I don't want a baby on my birthday...."

Amy: He said, "We can't have a summer baby because everybody's always out of town for birthdays." So that left us like, literally, four months that we could target to have a baby.

Trey: Little did we know....

Amy: Month after month after month of trying. Due dates went out the window; that didn't matter. It was just, *when*?

Trey: We got pregnant after about nine months of actively trying.

Amy: We were very excited. We went in for a first ultrasound—and there was no heartbeat. I knew it as soon as they did the scan.

Trey: The nurse tech said, "I'm not seeing anything. I think you'll need to talk to a doctor." So, they put us in a room and we sat there for ...

Amy: … an hour….

Trey: We were both freaking out about what was going on. We were thinking, maybe everything is still okay….?

Finally, the doctor came to tell us that this was not a viable pregnancy. We were totally crushed. We had waited so long and prayed so hard, and we'd thought it had finally worked.

We had to go through the whole D&C. It was all extremely scary.

Amy: And sad. We hadn't told anybody we had tried because we wanted the good news to be a surprise. Everyone dreams of making the fun announcement. Instead, we were calling to tell my parents and his parents that we'd miscarried.

Trey: They were crushed to hear the news. They tried to make us feel better by saying things like, "Miscarriage is so common. So many people have miscarriages…."

Amy: …and, "Something must have been wrong. This was God's way of taking care of it—of a baby that probably should not have been born."

Trey: We knew what they were saying was right—to a certain extent, but it didn't take away the pain.

Amy: We were still very hopeful. The very next cycle we were able to try, we got pregnant again. We were excited, but totally guarded. We saw a heartbeat. Then, when we came back in, the same tech started the ultrasound and immediately she got quiet. The room was silent. There was no heartbeat.

So, same story. We were put in a room, waited an hour to see the doctor, found out we had miscarried.

The kicker was that we were both in weddings that weekend. My best friend was getting married and his best friend was getting married, so we were headed to two different states. I didn't want to let my friend down, so I chose to wait until

Monday to have the D&C—praying all weekend that I wouldn't start miscarrying on my own as I was walking down the aisle. The whole thing was horrendous. That was the end of us trying naturally. We decided to go to a fertility specialist.

Trey: They seemed to have all the answers. They told us about something called PGD… pre-implantation genetic diagnosis. With IVF, they would be able to take an egg and the sperm and genetically test all of it—which we thought would be great.

We'd had our two miscarriages and maybe this was the answer.

Amy: In speaking with the doctor, it was very hard to imagine going from A to Z—with "A" being trying on our own with no medicine, no help and totally natural…, to "Z" being in vitro fertilization.

Trey: We had to go home and think about it.

Amy: But, I was so scared at that point of having another miscarriage that anything that could be done….

Trey: So, that's what we did next.

Amy: I injected myself every morning and every night. I went into the doctor every morning and after ten days, I went in for an ultrasound. My body was not responding. Despite very high levels of medicine, I was not producing the follicles needed to retrieve anything. They said, "It's no big deal."

Trey: So the months of waiting, all the shots, paying for all these medicines, all the plans we'd made that this was going to work and we'd get pregnant, thinking about when a baby would come… everything totally stopped.

Amy: At that point, we were feeling very impatient. I had friends around me who were getting pregnant left and right. We'd thought this was our answer.

Trey: During all this, Amy was attending at least four baby showers a month. Siblings were having babies left and right. Cousins. You name it. Everyone around us was pumping out babies and making it look easy.

Amy: We didn't want to tell everyone we were trying. At the time, we didn't have any friends who'd had any trouble conceiving. We were still 28 years old. In our world, there weren't many people facing this kind of difficulty... or, they weren't very open about it.

Trey: We didn't want people to think there was anything wrong with us. There's that stigma. We didn't want to add to our stress.

Our parents knew we were trying IVF and doing PGD. Although they were extremely supportive, they had mixed feelings about our decision. Amy's dad asked, "Why are you doing all this? It's going to happen naturally. You just need to be more patient." Meanwhile, our moms were game if it brought a baby into our arms.

Amy: The first day I was allowed to, I was trying again. We started a second IVF cycle, and it was a total repeat of the first— no follicles.

Then, on IVF Round #3, we tried an extra tweak of medicine. Lo and behold, picture perfect! Everything looked fantastic. We did a retrieval, they did the PGD testing and—five days later—we ended up with two healthy embryos to transfer.

The night before our blood test was done to see if the embryo implanted, we did something we probably shouldn't have: we decided to test at home. There was basically no line on the pregnancy test—a bare hint, faint positive—and my heart dropped. I remember crying myself to sleep.

Trey: It was only a chemical pregnancy; it had not taken. We didn't tell one single soul outside the family.

Everyone thought we were trying on our own, or not even necessarily trying. We'd just say, "We're thinking about it, but we're busy with work, too." It was very much a private thing.

By this time, we were definitely a mess. Through infertility, you figure out that this is out of your control. But, guys like to fix things...

Amy: ... especially Trey. He wanted to fix it for me. For us. It killed him to see me so upset.

Trey: I didn't come up with any solutions, but I certainly wanted to!

Amy: That was the hard thing for him. He was in a role where he could be supportive, but he couldn't fix it. The whole theme of our journey was a roller coaster of hope-fail-hope-fail-hope-fail-hope-fail.

We decided to try another IVF cycle because the chemical pregnancy was encouraging, in a way. Now, I look back at IVF and think I should have run, but at the time....

Trey: The doctors had a reason for everything. They'd say, "Oh, it would've worked, but we gave you too much Progesterone." Or, "You really needed a lower such-and-such level."

Amy: We jumped into the next cycle, did the exact same protocol, and it was total non-response. They cancelled my cycle, which was devastating because it just meant weeks of wasted time, effort and money.

At an ultrasound a week later, though, they said, "You are ready for a retrieval. Your body suddenly decided to respond." I had to wait another cycle to do a frozen transfer. It was crazy. The whole thing was crazy. And I got pregnant!

Then, a few weeks later, I started cramping. We determined I was definitely miscarrying. I had to have another D&C and cancel our vacation, which was another theme for us.... We could make no plans because of all these cycles.

That was a very low point because what had happened

was the antithesis of what we'd gone into this crazy medical reproductive world for—to *not* miscarry. And here I was having a more painful miscarriage than I'd ever had before.

Trey: Through everything that happened, we couldn't understand what was going on. Why was God doing this to us? I got angrier and angrier.

Amy: I felt sad, disappointed, upset, impatient....

Trey: All our prayers were to give our doctors the knowledge and ability to get us pregnant. When they failed on us or it didn't work, we thought we had to pray harder.

Amy: But at the time, what was the alternative?

Trey: I was angry at God. And we didn't understand: Why?! We sincerely wanted to be parents. We felt like we were ready. Why wasn't God ready for us to be parents?!

Amy: Trey thought that God must be punishing us because our life had been so good. We hadn't been tested.

Trey: We hadn't lost a parent or had a lot of painful events. And we were surrounded by friends who'd lost a father or had something else horrible happen. I thought maybe it was our turn.

Amy: It hurt to think that God could be saying, "You've had a great life so far, so here's a dose of bad." I was mad at God that He wouldn't give us a healthy baby. I couldn't understand: if He had the capability, why wouldn't He? Maybe He wasn't paying attention to us. Trey felt it was intentional on God's part; I just didn't understand.

So, fast forward.... In the Spring, we backed away from IVF and did an IUI cycle. I over-responded and we got pregnant with triplets. That was a big surprise, and a little bit of a shock.

Three weeks later, I started bleeding and went in and we found out I'd lost two of the three. But we still had "Baby B" holding on tightly. I was on bedrest, and it was a very rough pregnancy with lots of scares and bleeding along the way.

At 19½ weeks, my water broke and we were forced to deliver the baby, knowing that it would not survive. We went to the hospital and delivered a little baby boy. He was too small to give him a formal name, so we called him "Lovebug."

Trey: That was a huge turning point. That whole experience was definitely life-changing for us.

Amy: But, out of that extremely sad, very painful period came hope because he was 100% healthy, genetically. The reason we lost him, most likely, was a blood clot that caused the sac to rupture.

Before, it was a struggle to get pregnant, get the embryo to implant and get it to grow—be healthy from the very start. Now, finally, we had encouragement that it was possible to have a 100% healthy baby. That was a ray of hope in a time that was very, very sad.

Trey: A month after that, the doctors suggested using a gestational carrier. Amy and I had opposite reactions. I felt like this was absolutely the answer. I was extremely excited. I felt we'd been through everything—and I didn't want Amy to go through the pain of carrying, and possibly losing, another baby. Amy felt just the opposite.

Amy: God gave me this burning desire for being pregnant and delivering our baby, so although this solution did meet our biggest goal—to try to have a baby conceived by Trey and me—I didn't want to always have somebody else involved in something that's normally so intimate between a husband and wife.

And, there was denial on my part. I blamed myself for not being able to carry a baby to term, and yet, I wasn't ready to believe that I couldn't do it. I was scared to death to do it and have more bad news, but a little voice inside me kept saying, "I think I can, I think I can, I think I can."

Trey: But then, our sister-in-law offered to be our gestational carrier...

Amy: ...and it was such a sweet offer...

Trey: ...and so, after five months of legal work, counseling for all four of us, blood work and more, we were able to get started.

Amy: We transferred the embryos—and it was just a chemical pregnancy. Two days later, it was over. We were literally back at square one with nothing, and no idea where to go next.

That's when you joined the infertility Bible study?

Amy: Yes. The class introduced us to people going through similar circumstances. Instead of being at a baby shower with all my friends who were experiencing blissful happiness, I could talk to people who understood what I was going through. It was such a room full of unconditional love and support.

Trey: It was so refreshing to be led by someone who had been through it. We immediately knew that this was genuine. And it was encouraging to talk to someone who had gotten to the other side of it.

We bonded with other couples right away because we were basically going through a lot of the same emotional ups and downs. We could joke about all the stupid doctor stuff—it was either that, or cry. So we laughed...

Amy: ... and we cried. The great thing was that when you'd talk to friends from the group—people going through the same things—it was a different kind of comfort than you'd get from people who didn't understand.

Trey: I didn't have any friends who'd ever opened up about infertility, so I didn't have anyone to talk to. Going to the class, I knew that every one of those guys was experiencing the same thing I was.

And it's funny… looking back on it, it's not like we sat around and talked about it. We didn't have to talk about it all the time to know that there was that deep down pain, and we had that in common. We could talk about sports or a totally different subject, and yet know that we were on the same wavelength.

Amy: We had a lot of anger towards God. We needed to be able to focus on God's faithfulness, and on scripture… to be able to learn about stories in the Bible, and to learn that God doesn't ever leave your side… to know that God has a plan… in order to be able to hold on to our faith.

Trey: It was helpful to talk about "Where is God? Why is this happening?" I was completely, absolutely furious, and I didn't understand.

We were in No Man's Land. And when you're going through infertility, you cling onto whatever you can. It's important that what you cling onto is from the Bible.

One thing we heard in the group was that God would never give us more than we could handle. We definitely were at the point of not being able to handle any more. Another thing that resonated with me was hearing, "You are pregnant with hope."

Amy: We decided to switch doctors. The new doctor said, "Take Letrozole and Glucophage for this many days, then come in for an IUI." So, we did. A few weeks later, we had a positive pregnancy test. Every week after that, we had positive ultrasounds. It was the most uneventful, wonderful, nerve-wracking, scary but fabulous pregnancy. On December 5th…

Trey: … we got our December baby! The most important thing I learned about doctors through all this is that they are amazingly gifted, and God gives them their gifts to help others, but they're humans and they don't have all the answers. I think I personally put them on a pedestal as if they did. Over time, though, I started losing that faith in them.

Amy: It was God's timing. It was nothing special about any-thing we did, it was simply God's time.

What else did you learn through your infertility journey?

Amy: Never lose faith. I was pregnant with hope the whole time. I wanted to be pregnant with more than hope, but even at the lowest point, I always had hope.

I always knew that God put a love of children in my heart, so I knew I'd be a mom some day. Part of the process was learning to be open to however that happened. Because we were open to wherever God would lead us, I knew that somehow a child would come into our lives.

Trey: I will never understand the loss of our son. But I do think that we've grown stronger as a couple. We have been able to reach out to others—minister to others—which is a gift we wouldn't be able to give if we hadn't suffered ourselves.

And, we met incredible people along the way. Some of our best friends. We feel very blessed to know all the people who stood by us through our struggle.

Amy: I know now that when bad things happen, God cries with you. That helped me because when we were angry or I was so hurt, I didn't necessarily think He was doing bad things to us, but I wondered where He was. It made me feel better to know that God was hurting with me.

Trey: Another thing… your plan and timing may be very differ-ent from what God ultimately has in mind, but God *does* have a plan for your life. That includes having kids.

Amy: After our son was born, we decided to trust in whatever God wanted….

Trey: And, seven months later…

Amy: …I had an inkling that I should take a pregnancy test. I took it and it turned positive. Immediately.

Trey: When you think of all we have gone through, it is a total miracle to us that it happened. Two healthy sons. Truly, a total miracle.

Amy: And finally, a little confirmation for me, the eternal optimist. Timing and everything was part of that, but God had a plan.

Trey: I would do it all again to be where we are now.

Amy: I think we will always have the deepest appreciation for our children. We will not take them for granted. I will *never* put our boys to bed without a full heart.

Answering "Why?"

Ask any couple, "How did you two meet?" and after a moment's recollection, they will recount stories of initial attraction, subsequent wooing, and a growing desire for intimacy. Regardless of the current state of the relationship, every couple remembers traveling that familiar path toward a lifetime commitment.

For most, the memories are sweet—but, in the midst of this struggle, they seem increasingly distant. Infertility, and the stresses that accompany it, have altered the expected trajectory of a joyful life together, taking them into unfamiliar emotional and psychological territory.

As they have fought to maintain equilibrium in the midst of near-constant uncertainty, many partners admit they've gravitated toward one of two coping strategies. Either, they have pulled back as a self-protective defense mechanism. Or, at the other extreme, they have pushed for a boundary-invading nearness in search of constant reassurance.

Often, couples unconsciously use both strategies—with one spouse pushing away while the other pulls closer. The push-me-pull-you exhausts them both and threatens to undermine mutually-supportive intimacy.

As they have struggled to find some balance, most people find they have also withdrawn from the God who seems so absent and unresponsive. Consciously or not, they have allowed their feelings of isolation and unwelcome vulnerability to affect their spiritual lives.

Whatever attraction they once felt to God, they no longer seem able to find meaningful intimacy in their relationship with Him.

Like Job, each of us withstands as much as possible. But, endless struggle begins to undermine faith, making trust seem increasingly impossible.

Can we learn to see infertility from God's perspective? If so, might this new perspective alter our experience? In what ways? How soon? Armed with these urgent questions, we return to Job looking for answers.

> Many people withdraw from the God who seems so unresponsive

As we try to reframe the question "Why?" in terms of our learning from Job's experience, we quickly encounter two stumbling blocks. Both are rooted in common interpretations of Job's story.

First, Job's circumstances are frequently seen as a test of faith. A man previously awash in abundant blessings loses it all in a very brief span of time. With no explanation. Will he be able to sustain his faith? If he does, will he be rewarded? If he doesn't, will he be punished?

From this vantage point, Job's story has unnerving implications for us: (1) We may be required to prove our faith by suffering, (2) Like any test, a test of faith can be failed with unspecified negative consequences, (3) God's blessings may have to be earned, and therefore, (4) A cause-and-effect calcula-

•　　•　　•

Pause and consider…. Had any of these implications occurred to you? Which are most disconcerting—and why? Do they affect your willingness to trust God with your infertility?

•　　•　　•

tion appears to be at work in our relationship with God.

Truth be told, none of these implications gives us a bit of hope in the midst of infertility. *But*, we must remember that Job's story is part of the Old Testament. The life, death and resurrection of Jesus completely transformed the Old Testament covenant between God and His people.

The new covenant, the good news of the gospel found in the New Testament, replaces God's "obey me and prove yourselves, then I will bless you" with unmerited grace. A performance-based relationship has become one of unconditional love.

We are no longer required to earn blessings or prove ourselves worthy of abundance. We are made worthy by grace—not by passing tests. We are sanctified by faith in who Jesus is, and what he has done for us—not by our own successes or failures [Ephesians 2:8].

> We are free from the burden Job faced to earn God's blessing

In other words, we are free from the burden Job faced to prove his faithfulness by passing a test, in order to earn God's renewed blessing. We are made right with God through Jesus [John 3:16].

The result, then, is not that we must understand the test parameters and exceed God's expectations—like Job—if we want a child. There is no test. *We cannot, and do not need to, earn this blessing.* Instead, we are invited to accept the gift of Jesus himself as evidence of God's abundant love for us. Even as we have been unconsciously turning away from Him, God has pursued us with this incredible gift of love-inspired sacrifice [Romans 5:8].

●   ●   ●

Pause and consider... If there is no test and you can't earn this blessing, then what is God's role in your infertility?

●   ●   ●

God longs to bless us. Will we trust Him to do so?

Jesus said, "No one can come to the Father except through me" [John 14:6]. Clearly then, we must seek Jesus, draw near to him, and learn from him if we want to receive the gifts of God's grace and abundant blessings into our infertility experience.

As we draw nearer to Jesus, our mindfulness of his growing presence in our circumstances will begin to alter our perspective on them. The question is, *how*? This leads us to the second stumbling block in Job's story: the message that God is unknowable. Unfathomable. Incomprehensible. If this is true, how can we possibly hope to shift our perspective to one like His? Is it impossible, as Job concludes, to understand the mind of God?

Again, we must look to the New Testament and to Jesus' own words. He said plainly, "I and the Father are one heart and mind" [John 10:30, Message]. The words of Jesus were, and are, to be taken as direct-from-the-heart of God, the Father.

God is not unknowable; we know Him through Jesus

What he reveals about the plans, purpose, mind and will of God are intended to be understood by us. They begin to make God's perspective comprehensible to us because it is God's desire to be known and loved by us.

"...No one knows the Father except the Son," Jesus taught, "and those to whom the Son chooses to reveal Him" [Matthew 11:27]. Jesus was, and is, identifying himself as the primary revelation of God to mankind. He simultaneously points to our limited understanding, and to himself as the means of understanding. He is showing us the path to meaningful communion with the God who longs to be revealed to His people.

"...I do nothing on my own," Jesus declared, "but speak just what the Father has taught me. The one who sent me is with me; he has not left me alone, for I always do what pleases him"

[John 8:28-29]. Jesus was, and is, commenting on his intimate relationship with God—and reassuring us that he is, therefore, able to speak for Him to us. Jesus' words and actions can always be trusted to reveal the thoughts and heart of God.

Jesus further described his role in our relationship with God: "As the Father has loved me, so have I loved you. Now remain in my love" [John 15:9]. His directions are simple and clear: see me as evidence of the depth and strength of God's love, and remain in that love in order to be intimate with the Father.

"I am the way, and the truth, and the life. No one comes to the Father except through me. If you really knew me, you would know my Father as well" [John 14:6-7]. These words of Jesus are the promise and the invitation. The unfathomable God of Job's story is revealed through Jesus Christ. So, the implications of Job's story *for us* must be reconsidered in light of Christ's offer to enter into a deep, meaningful relationship *with us*—one which enables us to know the mind and will of God.

Unlike Job, we are not expected to trust a God we cannot begin to understand. God longs for us to see clearly who He is and how much He loves us. Jesus is the way—to see clearly what has been invisible, to understand what has seemed incomprehensible, to shift our perspective on infertility to God's perspective, and ultimately, to renew our intimacy with the One whom we *can* know and trust.

●　　●　　●

Pause and consider…. Does all of this seem intuitive to you? Irrelevant? Irrational? Why do you think you feel this way? How are your feelings affecting your ability to understand God's role in your infertility story? Is it possible for them to change? Then, what might happen…?

●　　●　　●

Both of the stumbling blocks in Job's story point us toward Jesus. So, now we must bring our desire to understand our experience from God's perspective to him.

Did Jesus have anything specific to say about suffering? Do any of his teachings have direct implications for our infertility experience and our longing to understand? The answer is, emphatically, *yes*!

Jesus clearly understood the human need to ask, "Why?" He also recognized the natural inclination to presume cause-and-effect, and to place ourselves at the center of our perspective. Many of the lessons he taught exposed this predisposition, and then turned it on its head in order to manifest God's perspective.

> Jesus clearly understood the need to ask "why?" in response to suffering

As we study Jesus' words and actions in the Bible—and then consider their implications for us—we can see more and more clearly from God's perspective.

We begin with the story of a miracle and the question that accompanied it [John 9:1-3]. The disciples encountered a man who was blind since birth and immediately assumed that someone was to blame. Curious, they asked Jesus, "Who sinned?" In other words, they wanted to know: Whose fault is it—the blind man's parents', or his own?

The disciples presumed they knew *why* already. The common belief at the time was that sin results in suffering—so, suffering was considered transparent evidence of wrongdoing. The unspoken corollary was that suffering was God's preferred method of sin-deterrence. It kept people who wanted to avoid suffering motivated to avoid sin.

But, the story tells us the man had been blind from birth. Would God condemn a man for a sin before it was even committed? Would He punish an innocent man for life, just because his parents had once done wrong? The implications of the disciples' assumptions were—and are—deeply disturbing, in part because they are viscerally familiar. We, too, have sometimes wondered, "Whose fault is this infertility? Where does the blame lie? Is this punishment? For what?"

Jesus healed the man—who fully regained his sight—and then responded to the disciples' question. "Neither this man nor his parents sinned," said Jesus, "but this happened so that the work of God might be displayed in his life" [John 9:3].

Jesus completely upended the disciples' thinking. He changed the question from "who sinned?" to "why did this happen?"—and then he told them why: so that the work of God might be displayed in this life.

● ● ●

Pause and consider.... Does Jesus' teaching—"this happened so that the work of God might be displayed in this life"—surprise you? What does it make you think about your own suffering? Does it alter your perspective in any way?

● ● ●

Have you ever seen an apparent tragedy set the stage for God's dramatic intervention? What were the circumstances and the outcome of that story? Are you willing to consider that such a thing could happen to you?

● ● ●

Jesus' answer to the disciples' question, "Who sinned?" incorporated several informative responses to the *right* question, "Why did this happen?"

The first reason it happened was to enable sight—the literal sight of the blind man, and the figurative "sight" of the disciples. These students of Jesus' needed to "see" hardship and suffering in a completely different way, from God's grace-filled perspective.

Witnessing the blind man's healing, then hearing Jesus'

explanation for why it occurred, opened the disciples' eyes to new possibilities and a new understanding of how God redeems suffering—*by using its transformation to manifest His love.*

The second reason this happened was to create a teachable moment. Jesus had the undivided attention of the disciples. First, he surprised them by saying, "no one sinned," and then he shifted their focus from the blind man's suffering to God's grace.

He helped them "see" that blindness was not the story. It merely set the stage... laid the groundwork... and awaited the miracle. It was the necessary precursor to a blessing that completely transformed the man's circumstances. Without the blindness, the man might not have "seen" God's grace so clearly, or been so grateful for the gift of sight. This, then, is another way in which God redeems suffering—*by using it to help us "see" and appreciate grace.*

● ● ●

Suffering can help us "see" and appreciate God's grace

● ● ●

The third reason this happened was to glorify God. He was glorified when Jesus performed the miracle—since no man could do such a thing apart from God. He was also glorified when the newly-sighted man told his incredible story to group after group of listeners: "That someone opened the eyes of a man born blind has never been heard of— ever. If this man didn't come from God, he wouldn't be able to do anything" [John 9:32-33, Message].

This, then, is another way in which God redeems suffering—*by converting it into amazing experiences that make for compelling testimony, which honors and glorifies Him.*

With his brief but comprehensive answer to the disciple's question, Jesus helps us "see," just as he did the blind man. We are that man, in a sense—previously unable to see what was right in front of us, but now suddenly able to see clearly.

The disciples put an assumption of wrongdoing at the center of the question "Who...?" And, they assumed cause-and-effect. But Jesus teaches us to see that an assumption of grace belongs at the center. From there, the question "Why?" leads straight to the answer: *so that the work of God might be displayed in this life.*

This is good news for those of us who can't stop asking, "Why?" It directs us toward a new, grace-centered perspective, one from which any circumstances can be seen as providing the raw materials for a miracle that points to God.

●   ●   ●

Pause and consider.... What do you think about a grace-centered perspective? Do you believe this is God's vantage point on your experience? Could it to become yours, too? What might that change for you?

●   ●   ●

Another part of what we see through this story is that suffering is not always-and-only a curse. It also sets the stage for miracles. The experience of grief, loss or pain is never welcome, but God can redeem it—and He promises to [Romans 8:28]. The possibility of a pending miracle, and the promise of God's active role, can bring us peace in the present *if* we are willing to trust that what we have seen in the blind man's story applies to our lives, too.

This is good news for those of us who are suffering. We can will ourselves to sidestep the frequent temptations to dwell on our misery. Instead, we can look forward to the moment when the tide will turn as God redeems our experience—the moment when impossible will become possible, when God's seed of hope will become a kept promise, and our dream will become reality.

Through the blind man's story, Jesus teaches us to see more clearly who God is and what He can and will do—His power, His love, His compassion. Jesus teaches us that God transforms suffering from a curse into a pending blessing—one which becomes a foundation for faith and a cause for joy.

When we decide to apply this expectation to our own experience, we discover we need to rephrase the question "Why?" to incorporate an assumption of grace. When we do, the question changes from a petulant "Why?!" to one seeking insight from the God of grace: "Why, *if you love me and intend to redeem this experience*, are you saying, No, God?"

Voiced this way, the question allows for all sorts of grace-based answers:

- Because this egg or sperm won't make the child I have planned for you.
- Because I want you to mature and gain wisdom first.
- Because you don't trust Me yet, but you need to.
- Because I intend for you to benefit from something else first.
- Because I am strengthening your faith, your patience and your perseverance.
- Because your priorities are still shifting into place.
- Because you need to deal with something else first—something I know is coming.
- Because your heart isn't ready; you need time to heal and recover.
- Because I want you to adopt instead.
- Because the child you'll be adopting hasn't even been conceived yet.
- Because I'm still setting the stage for this miracle.
- Because I want the best for you; so, it's not time—yet.

Whatever the specific reason, the common denominator in all these grace-based answers is "Yes, but…." Can you hear the "Yes"? God recognizes our deep hunger for a child. He planted the seed of hope that has sustained the desire for so long. When He says, "Yes, but not yet," He means, "Yes, I know you want this child now, but you will need to wait *if you want My best*."

Is that what we want: God's very best? Can we trust

Him enough to wait for it? Or, like Sarah, do we feel compelled to keep pushing?

Clearly, God's plan is not our plan—because our plan would happen NOW. But, every reason He says "No," or "Not yet" comes out of His love for us. Even if it doesn't seem, feel or look like it—and even if we don't know "*Why* not now?"—it is safe to assume that God is in the process of blessing us. It is already in the works [Matthew 6:32-33].

The Bible advises us, therefore, to "…fix our eyes not on what is seen, but on what is unseen. For what is seen is temporary, but what is unseen is eternal" [II Corinthians 4:18]. God's faithfulness is promised and proven repeatedly throughout the Bible. It will be proven in our lives, too. But, now we must wait.

In the meantime, we can do two things. First, we can begin modifying our questions, thoughts and actions to reflect an assumption of God's faithfulness—an acknowledgement of His grace, as revealed to us by Jesus. As we do, we will begin to shift from our old, self-centered perspective to God's grace-centered one. This will profoundly alter what we see and feel.

● ● ●

While we wait, we can change our perspective, and ask new and better questions

● ● ●

Second, we can begin leaning into our growing knowledge of God's plans and purpose—allowing that knowledge to soothe our spirits, and open our own hearts to these new questions: What are you wanting to teach me, God? How are you maturing me and making me wiser? How are you molding my experience to make me a better parent? How are you preparing my heart to be more grateful? How are you renewing my mind to be more like Jesus? What do you want to accomplish in and through me during this time of waiting? All these questions can be asked, and answers received, if we have a truly open heart and mind.

When we come to this new perspective, we will begin to *see*—for the first time—how our infertility experience may actually, ultimately, be a blessing-in-disguise. This is not a concept that is easy to embrace; prolonged suffering has left deep wounds. But it is one that Jesus is leading us toward as we continue on our spiritual journey.

The lessons to come will bring us more, richer insights that will—one day—make it possible to affirm the Bible's promise: "…waiting does not diminish us, any more than waiting diminishes a pregnant mother. We are enlarged in the waiting. We, of course, don't see what is enlarging us. But the longer we wait, the larger we become, and the more joyful our expectancy" [Romans 8:22-23, Message].

●　　●　　●

Pause and consider…. Could your infertility possibly be a blessing-in-disguise? This can be a very emotionally-charged question for those hoping (and struggling) to conceive. What do you think or feel about it? Has this lesson changed anything for you?

●　　●　　●

Reflections

Robin & Don

How did your story begin?

Don: I met Robin when I was 43, and she was 41. We got introduced on a blind date. We knew pretty soon that we were going to get married.

Robin: We both knew one thing we had in common was a real love for family. We also had a desire, dating way back, to be parents—so, we hoped that would be in our future.

Don: I thought, realistically, that at this point, the chances of me being able to be a father were pretty slim. I remember telling some friends one time that that would be my biggest disappointment in life....

Robin: You told me that. If you were never a dad, it would be your biggest disappointment. And, you told me you'd always dreamed of raising sons.

Don: I came from a family with all boys.

Robin: I really felt the call to be a mom and I knew Don would be a wonderful dad. We decided to try getting pregnant the old-fashioned way. We got pregnant twice, but with my age, the chances of miscarriage were higher. Neither pregnancy lasted very long—just five or six weeks. There was a good two-year period where we tried and were not successful.

It was hard. It was hard to think that we had passed the point of being fertile and being able to have our own biological children.

Don: We talked to fertility specialists… went to two sessions with doctors… and somehow, we just weren't at peace with that approach. It just didn't hit us right. Not as in Right and Wrong— just that we weren't sure it was right *for us*. I was probably stronger on that than Robin was.

Robin: I don't know, honey. With my Catholic upbringing….

Don: We just never got comfortable with in vitro. But again, in no way am I judgmental of folks who use that approach. It's just that for us, I saw a crossroads that I might have trouble with… How many? What do you do with extra eggs? Do you freeze them? And then what? All that sort of stuff.

I thought, maybe I'm not mature enough to deal with those issues. I think I'd rather avoid facing those choices and pursue another approach.

Robin: We realized the natural way was probably not going to work for us, and I thought adoption would be a wonderful thing.

Don: That possibility had never crossed my mind. Not because I was opposed to it, but just because I didn't have any close friends who had done it. I had two cousins who were adopted, but in the "old school" of adoption—where you didn't ever talk about it. They just joined the family as infants, and you didn't talk about where they came from.

Robin: I knew that there were children out there who needed homes, and we had so much love to give. We wanted that meaning in our lives; we wanted a family of our own. It was a real strong drive for both of us.

When we talked about adoption…

Don: … I wanted to go slowly there, too. I wasn't initially committed and convinced that that was the right approach for us.

Robin: We had to think through being older parents. How did we feel—if we adopted only one—about raising an only child? We were trying to put ourselves in the child's shoes. And that was hard, because we both have siblings and loved the idea of our child having a sibling.

What made you decide to join the infertility Bible study?

Robin: I had gone to a few infertility/adoption support group meetings in my neighborhood. A neighbor—who had been through the infertility Bible study—made a point of saying, "I would love for you to try the group at church." So, we made it a point to do that.

It was so good because I was doing what women do—making it a point to talk to other women, get information, research possibilities, find resources, learn about adoption. But it's not as easy for husbands to do that.

Having a chance to initiate Don into being with other couples who were exploring adoption or other avenues… it was great to do that as a couple. It helped us continue to move forward—to kind of put ourselves out there as a couple starting to look at how to grow our family.

Don: Coming to the group was very easy for me. It didn't take any serious discussions to make that happen. It was as much for me as for Robin.

Robin: We were just a couple weeks into thinking adoption was the path we were probably going to pursue….

Don: I have to say that I was thinking if, for whatever reason, I got cold feet or adoption didn't feel right, we could stop the presses.

Robin: And that was right when we came to the first class.

Don: I knew there was great value in small groups. Robin and I just hadn't had a chance yet to find a small group where we both felt a fit. This seemed like a great way to meet people and connect with them.

Robin: The class had us talking about things every week. It had us thinking. It brought this all front and center for us, which was very important.

It was also very helpful to be around other couples on different paths, but all with the goal of having a family and sharing in that desire. We were reminded that there are a lot of different ways of becoming parents. What's key is the child who becomes part of your family at the end of it.

Don: I can look back on it now as a Monday morning quarterback. I'm one who believes God's touch is very subtle. You've got to exert immense patience to understand—and wait for—what He's doing in your life. There can be struggles, joys… but if you immediately jump to a conclusion about what they mean, you may miss the longer-term message.

When we couldn't get pregnant, I wondered, has God sent us a message? We have not been able to get pregnant. Is there a message there? What we know is that doctors tell us, "We can go in and manipulate things and get you pregnant. If you guys want a baby, we'll get you a baby via advanced methods."

I say, hooray for advanced medicine and all the smart people who can make that happen, but I was listening and thinking, is God saying, "You shouldn't be parents?" Or, "You should take another approach?" Robin and I would talk about that. Or, are we the two siblings in our family who are destined to take care of our aging parents because the other siblings have children…?

Robin: I would say one more thing about the class. It was very supportive to know that other couples are praying for you. You're reminded that God is in charge and having that focus every week—and praying for others during the week—it helped relieve some stress and anxiety for me.

From the beginning, we felt the love and caring from the other couples. We felt the support and encouragement, and that was very positive. But also, from the first lesson on, learning and remembering that I didn't have to figure it all out was great. I needed a prayerful focus that God was in control, and the class really helped me.

Don: I look back on it now, and I see that what God was doing during this time was holding us off. The timing needed to be just right.

I guess if I was going to speak with other infertile couples, I'd say, "Don't sit back and wait for it all to come to you, but be patient with how quickly you jump into something because God's got opportunities and messages there for you. You've got to be listening. You can't just take over your own life and say, 'I know what I'm going to do. My friends are saying do this, and my family is saying do that.'

The messages are subtle and you need to stay connected to your faith. *Really* stay connected to your faith."

Robin: We chose an adoption agency that was recommended by a friend in the neighborhood. We liked the Christian basis and that it was a sound organization. The way they did business... we liked all of that.

Don: Our process with them was helpful for me because it gave me a chance to understand some things. Normally, you bond with the pregnant mother and take the infant home with you from the hospital. I needed to know how that happens. How is everybody supported emotionally? Are these babies being sold into the market? Are the moms doing this willingly? Are they getting paid for these babies? Are the moms making good, no-pressure decisions? I needed to know that this was all happening in a way that was spiritually sound.

Robin: Meanwhile, we worked on our profile. It was twelve pages of photos and text, and it turned out well. We were told to expect a 12-18 month wait until we were matched and could get a child. No guarantees, though.

Don: That was a struggle for us because we'd put in all this effort, and then we hit a wall. We couldn't do anything but wait for the phone to ring.

Robin started getting antsy. Our profile wasn't in for a week and she was saying, "I'm not sure we're with the right agency. Maybe we need another agency." I asked Robin to give it a few months to see if something happened.

Robin: It was a control thing for me. Because of our age, we didn't want to wait—so, should we widen our net? We'd had our profile with them for 10 days when we got a phone call.

Don: My cell phone rang and I saw the name of the adoption agency. My heart just dropped.

Robin: They'd said, "A phone call could be a match."

Don: So, when I saw the caller ID, I ignored it. I decided to let them leave a message. That was my control thing. Thirty minutes later, Robin called me and I had a feeling something was going on.

Robin: I get chills thinking about it. I was out-of-state on business. The social worker called me. When I answered, she asked, "Are you ready to be blown away?"

Don: This is where the miracle starts. Robin called me. Having just received a call from the agency, I said, "Are you sitting down?" Then she said, "Are *you* sitting down?!"

Robin: I told him, "There is a birth mother with 5-month-old twin boys. She has been wanting to make an adoption plan since she was pregnant, but she's had a lot of false starts and has not followed through. Now, she's ready to go through with it."

Don: She was a single mom who quit working when she had the children and she was without resources, relying solely on charity. She needed to move, she needed to work…

Robin: … and she was ready to get this done. She wanted to place these children in the next 3-4 days, but she also wanted to meet us first. We said, "We're very interested and would love to meet her." So, having just driven to my meeting, I turned around and drove four hours home. We lay in bed that night staring at the ceiling.

Don: We met the boys and the mother the next day. The boys were beautiful and healthy… the things you wish for, but don't say out loud. To see them laugh and smile was just terrific, but at the same time, it all felt so sudden.

Robin: We talked about whether we could help her. Did she feel pressured? Did she just need some help? Was this a desperation decision for her?

Don: We asked the agency if we could provide her a financial lifeline for a couple months, so she could get to know us with no pressure. The agency, disappointingly, said, "That violates adoption protocol because it could be perceived as coercion. We can't allow it."

I asked if we could arrange something through our church. They told us, "No." So, it came back to us needing to make a decision.

Robin: She wanted a Christian family, an involved dad, a stay-at-home mom. She wanted her children not to have to struggle. She felt we were the right couple for her. We are just so thankful that she made such an unselfish decision.

So, what did you learn through your infertility experience?

Don: We want to recognize God's role in the timing of this miracle. It took us six months just to be qualified, and guess what? During that time, this mother—on four or five occasions —pursued an adoption plan and got cold feet and stopped. Now, she was starting again.

Here's the miracle: if we'd been ready six months earlier, this mom wouldn't have been ready. If we had been ready six months later, we might have missed adopting these boys.

God has a way of moving all the pawns around so that it's a win-win for everybody. This mom needed relief, these boys needed a home, Robin and I wanted children... and God worked it all out perfectly. In His perfect timing.

Robin: I'd add that I learned there are lots of blessings God will bring into your life. There's not just one set pattern, one path to get where you want to go. It's important to remember that there are so many different ways to live a happy, full life—and have children.

Don: It sounds formulaic, but trust God. Trust. God. There were probably some times when we tried to manage the situation, or the opportunities, or the circumstances. Watch that. Use the patient approach. Let it come to you. Be ready and do your part. But let it come on God's time.

Discovering Peace

Sometimes, a particular insight or idea will resonate with someone in our group as nothing else ever has. This happened for one husband shortly after we began discussing the idea of shifting to a new perspective.

Joe had been participating in our infertility study group for weeks, but had never said a word. He'd come, originally, to support his wife, Nancy, in a way that she would find meaningful. Session after session, he would sit completely silent and still —showing neither interest nor boredom... never angry, never sad. There was no outward sign that anything we discussed was registering.

Then one day, he spoke.

He said that the grace-filled perspective we'd been discussing—one that somehow changes what you see and how you experience infertility—was real. He'd made the discovery in a conversation with a friend. The two men had joined several others for a ski weekend. They'd all seen each other a year before for a similar event. His friend commented that this year, the husband from our group seemed "lighter." More at peace. More comfortable with his life.

The amazing thing, he told us, was that by the world's standards, his life had taken a dramatic turn for the worse. He'd changed jobs—which added stress to an already stressful work life. His father had recently died. And, both Nancy and her father had just been diagnosed with cancer. On top of all that, they were struggling with infertility—the medications, the miscarriages, failed IUI's and more recently, an unsuccessful IVF. By all the usual measures, he should have been considerably less peaceful than a year before.

"But, my friend was right," he said with conviction. "I realized when he said it that, even though we don't know what's going to happen, I feel better than I used to because I know God is in this with us." He continued, "Our circumstances are worse than a year ago, but I've got a lot more peace."

> "I know God is in this with us; I've got a lot more peace."

Nancy had listened to the story with her head bowed. Now, tears streaking her face, she took his hand and they looked at us, waiting for the group's response.

It was the first time someone had shared such a powerful "aha" moment—when spiritual principles we'd been discussing had intersected with their day-to-day reality, and the truth had become crystal clear.

The story had an amazing, galvanizing effect on the group. Here was evidence of God at work! This man's circumstances hadn't improved; in fact, he made clear they'd gotten worse. And yet, his willingness to invite God into the midst of this chaotic life—and respond to His guidance—had profoundly altered his experience of those circumstances.

The peace he described, found in the midst of a tornado of tragic events, was what everyone in the group was searching for. And now, here was tangible evidence that it could actually be found.

The story encouraged the whole group—in several ways. First, it affirmed the content of our studies, along with their impact. Second, it provided evidence of a meaningful transformation in Joe's life, which made that possibility more powerfully real to everyone. Third, it provided an unsolicited assessment of the effect of a transformation (i.e., it was obvious to someone outside our infertility group). And best of all, it provided hope.

If someone mired in all those tragic experiences could find genuine peace, then there was hope for everyone.

●　　●　　●

Pause and consider.... Does Joe's spontaneous testimony strike you as reasonable, or is it unimaginable? Predictable, or unexplainable? Why do you feel this way?

●　　●　　●

Does his story give you hope that a similar transformation could occur in your own life, or your spouse's? If not, why? If so, what would that change for you?

●　　●　　●

By his own admission, Joe had never envisioned giving testimony to God's faithfulness—not to this group, or any other. And certainly not *before* all these tragedies released their hold on his life. But, here he was affirming the truth of our discussions, along with their impact on his life.

This was not a situation-dependant peace he was experiencing. Just the opposite. This was independent of all the challenges he was facing.

In the Bible, the apostle Paul writes, "I consider that our present sufferings are not worth comparing with the glory that will be revealed in us" [Romans 8:18]. That glory is the transforming work of God, achieved when our powerlessness humbles us, making way for the power of the Holy Spirit to change us.

When we stop resisting God—and enthroning ourselves—and instead, acknowledge our limits, we open the door for the Holy Spirit to enter our lives.

"I can't fix this, God... you can change me or change

my circumstances, but I'm at the end of my rope." When we reach the end of ourselves, and realize we are open to a new, deeper relationship with God, the transformation begins.

This is exactly what happened in Joe's life. Struggling under the weight of so much adversity, he acknowledged his limitations (to himself, if not to anyone else). He agreed to attend our Bible study and a men's prayer breakfast—even if he did not actively participate or expect much in the way of results.

And then, by choosing to immerse himself in God's word and opening himself to God's transforming power, he tapped into a reservoir of living water [John 7:38]. He found something that renewed him. More than that, it strengthened him and began to change him—from the inside, out.

● ● ●

He discovered how to tap into a reservoir of living water

● ● ●

How did that happen?

Even after hearing his story, many couples still seemed uncertain. What about Joe's experience could enlighten them? Can anything about it help you? Can any of us tap into the same reservoir of living water that brought him such peace?

We begin to answer these questions by looking at a critically important choice all of us must make.

Many of us choose to live our lives with one foot planted in each of two worlds. Monday through Saturday (and much of Sunday), we live in what we think of as "the real world." It's a world populated by self-reliant souls—like us all striving for success and recognition.

On Sunday morning, we are reminded of "the spiritual world" where the striving is redirected in service to others, for the Kingdom of God. Many of us find that selflessness appealing, but also somewhat unrealistic to maintain 24/7—if we intend to succeed by "real world" standards.

Straddling these two worlds, we do our best to make sense of their inconsistencies—generally, on an as-needed basis.

Resolving their differences is not urgent because we expect these two worlds to remain distinctly separate. *But, suffering changes that.*

With infertility, we become painfully aware of the real world's inability to make sense of our suffering. The question "why?" finds no satisfying answers. We discover that the Kingdom of Me is powerless to force resolution. We cannot will relief of our suffering into place any more than we can will a heartbeat into the womb. Citizenship in this kingdom only seems to bring with it increasing isolation, loneliness, fear, anxiety, and obsession over the loss of control.

●   ●   ●

Pause and consider.... Does "the real world's inability to make sense of suffering" resonate with you? What parts of your infertility journey have been made more difficult by real world pressure or pretense?

●   ●   ●

Meanwhile, the spiritual world makes increasing sense to us. The Bible talks to us about suffering and blessing—and the words of comfort, understanding and peace resonate deep within us. Jesus teaches about the Kingdom of God and the presence of the Holy Spirit, and we hunger for the peace that comes with belonging to this world. Peace that transcends circumstances. Peace that is found in the flow of God's will, and the constancy of His love. Not just on Sunday, but every day.

When infertility drives these two worlds apart, we stretch to keep a foot in each world, while maintaining some semblance of balance. But, we can't sustain this stance for long.

As our two worlds move further and further apart—their differences standing in increasingly stark contrast to one another —we come to the moment when we must choose. In that critical moment, we step toward one world, and away from the other.

Some of us see the moment of choice approaching. Others, like Joe, see it more clearly in hindsight. Either way, the moment comes—and we say "yes" to self, or "yes" to God.

If we step toward the Kingdom of Me, we choose to struggle on under our own power. Our need for control has outmatched our spirit's cry for comfort. The internal pressure will continue to build, though, for as long as we fail to realize our dream. And, God may allow our circumstances to worsen—driving our worlds ever further apart—in order to call us to a greater awareness of our need for Him, and an opportunity to make another choice.

By contrast, when we step toward the Kingdom of God, we (re)affirm the meaning of our citizenship, our belonging, our place as God's beloved children. We choose the reality of faith over the illusion of control, the power of God over the weakness of self, and peace over fear.

> Ironically, we win the battle for peace by surrendering

We discover that by surrendering our fight to keep a foot in each world, we are victorious. We have won the all-important battle for peace in the midst of our circumstance. How? By surrendering.

This is what Joe had described.

How had he come to his moment of choice? He said it had become increasingly clear to him that—surprisingly—the time spent with our group was consistently the best hour of each week. When he and his wife were with us, they felt understood, inspired and comforted. Their hope was restored—again and again—by insights gained through our discussion.

The same thing was happening for him each week in the men's prayer breakfast. He felt encouraged, uplifted, and genuinely understood. Increasingly, he and his wife both had a sense of the Holy Spirit at work in their lives—teaching them through their circumstances, renewing their faith, and redeeming their suffering.

Although he was overwhelmed at times by challenges he faced in every part of his life, he was also increasingly at peace. Ever more uncertain of when or how he might become a father, he found himself increasingly willing to trust God's timing. Never before one to discuss God's kingdom, he was increasingly eager to tell others about his experience and the change occurring in his life.

He was victorious, despite the world's view of his circumstances, because he had found peace that did not depend on them.

●   ●   ●

Pause and consider.... Can you imagine feeling victorious despite your circumstances? Experiencing peace that is not situation-dependant? What leads you to say "yes" or "no"?

●   ●   ●

The Bible tells us that Jesus promised this peace to his disciples, saying, "Peace I leave with you; my peace I give you. *I do not give you as the world gives*" [John 14:27, italics added]. The peace of Christ. The peace that passes understanding. It is a peace available only through the Kingdom of God.

How does this kind of peace come into a life? The apostle Paul gives us the answer. He writes, "It's wonderful what happens when Christ displaces worry at the center of your life" [Philippians 4:7, Message]. That is the source of peace: Christ displacing worry at the center of your life.

●   ●   ●

Pause and consider.... Can you envision Christ displacing worry at the center of your life? Why, or why not?

●   ●   ●

Christ displacing worry means a new focus—not on worry, but on trust. And, a new perspective—centered on grace, embodied in Jesus.

It is a step away from self and toward God that enables a new way of seeing, one that is not situation-dependent. This is what it means to live in the Kingdom of God—not just Sunday mornings, but 24 hours a day, 7 days a week, 365 days a year.

When we abandon the Kingdom of Me, having seen all that it isn't and can never be, and we say a soul-deep *"yes"* to the Kingdom of God, we find our new center. We regain our equilibrium, despite everything that threatens to throw us off balance.

When we say "yes" to a Christ-centered life, we find lasting peace

When we plant both feet in this world, we are able to find rest—in the peace Jesus promised, the love of God that casts out fear, and hope that does not disappoint us [John 14:27, I John 4:18, Romans 5:5].

With this lesson, the disguised blessing of infertility begins to come into clearer focus. Eyes open to a new reality. Everything about infertility has brought us here: the loss, the grief, the pain, the isolation, the emptiness, the longing, the hunger, the need. It has brought each of us to this Bible study, to this lesson, to this moment of realizing that a choice must be made. And to this growing certainty that the Kingdom of God... is home.

Do dramatic transformations take place in the life of everyone who participates in our group? A new sort of hope *does* take root midway through the course.

Consider this evidence.

Many couples begin sensing a new desire to seek God and His grace-filled perspective. For some, the blessing in that is the genuineness of their desire (rather than a sense of obligation they may have felt in the past). For others, the focus on grace is a welcome relief from constant thoughts of failure and loss.

Some couples realize limitations they initially resented have led them to a place of humility. They begin to recognize the truth of the Bible axiom, "...God opposes the proud, but gives grace to the humble" [I Peter 5:5]. Less self-reliance and insistence on control results in growing God-reliance. They sense God beginning to work with them, in them, through them—and that leads them to greater peace.

Other couples begin to see that infertility is a way for God to gain their undivided attention. Previously, they may have been too busy with other, higher priorities. They often acknowledge having had little interest in day-to-day intimacy with God.

Now, humbled by their obvious helplessness, they find themselves returning to Him, newly cognizant of their need for His compassion, mercy and grace. Thankfully, He welcomes them home like prodigal children.

Couples also begin to see that the Bible's promise of "hope and a future" might grow out of this spiritual journey. Rather than resenting it, they start to see the benefit of a period of spiritual growth and relationship renewal prior to becoming parents.

> • • •
>
> **Couples see that hope and a future might grow out of this spiritual journey**
>
> • • •

They are building community, as well, with their fellow travelers. These relationships become richer with each week's shared discoveries. This, too, is a sign of hope and a future.

Taken all together, it is quite a collection of evidence. Clearly, God wasn't just at work one time, in the life of one man. He is at work in the life of every infertile couple that allows Him to enter into their story.

Why don't couples see this sooner? Maybe because a part of "seeing" is looking for... anticipating... expecting. In the beginning, most infertile couples are looking for nothing more than temporary relief from suffering. *This* is so much more.

Interestingly, in the Bible, it is the righteous—God's loved and chosen ones—who struggle with infertility. This fact surprises and puzzles many infertile couples. Why would that be? Why would God's favorites be compelled to suffer?

The answer is because, rather than a curse, infertility is repeatedly revealed to be a precursor to miraculous events. Transformations occur in the lives of the parents-to-be, preparing them to steward extraordinary children. Then, their miracle children go on to lead God's people in history-changing ways.

This is true in the stories of Sarah, Rebekah, Rachel, Hannah and Elizabeth. They all struggled with infertility, and then gave birth to children who served God well by shepherding His people [Genesis 18, Genesis 25, Genesis 29, I Samuel, Luke 1].

These Bible stories show us, repeatedly, that infertility is often just the opposite of what it appears to be in the world's eyes: not a curse, but a blessing-in-the-works.

Might it be that God has chosen to continue this pattern of infertility being just the opposite of what it appears, right into the present? Might each of the couples in our groups (and each of those reading this book) be at the beginning of a miraculous experience? Might this "affliction" be a temporary means by which God will achieve a sacred end?

Absolutely.

●　●　●

Pause and consider.... Could infertility be a precursor to something miraculous in *your* life? Do you see evidence of God transforming you, or your spouse—preparing you to steward an extraordinary child? Are you willing to trust God's timing and His purposefulness?

●　●　●

How can infertility be a means to a sacred end? Each

couple's miracle story might be the conception and birth of a new, life-changing relationship with God. It might be the story of a child's arrival in the life of their family. It might be a special calling of God on the life of that child. Or, it might be all of these.

Looking at infertility from this vantage point makes it seem less like a curse, and more like a well-disguised blessing. Will such a blessing come? Into every couple's life?

Anxiety keeps a strong grip on most infertile couples, even as they participate in our group. But Paul's words give hope and confident direction: "It's wonderful what happens when Christ displaces worry at the center of your life" [Philippians 4:7, Message].

Is this truly possible for any and every couple? Is it as simple as saying "yes" to God and awaiting the miracle? Or is there more that we can, or should, be doing during this time of waiting?

We want to keep moving forward—drawing nearer to God and wrestling with our fears—without tumbling back into the emotional and psychological pitfalls that are our familiar enemies. Is that possible? We bring these questions to our next discussion and dig into the Bible for answers.

Reflections

Nancy & Joe

How did your story begin?

Joe: Until we met, we were happily independent, didn't-need-another-person-to-complete-our-lives single people. Then, we met one another and realized we were wrong. We got married in 2002.

Nancy: I was 31. Joe was 30.

Joe: Early on in the marriage, we were convinced we did not want or need children. We thought of ourselves as a happy-go-lucky married couple who could go anywhere we wanted to whenever we wanted to—which we did.

Over time, I don't think there was any one event that triggered "we have to have children now." We were just so happy together, and we loved each other so much, that we felt we could share the love with someone else.

Nancy: We both went into the marriage saying we didn't want children, but if either one of us changed our mind then we'd be open to it.

Joe: So, we decided to start trying. Six months after that, Nancy was diagnosed with cervical cancer.

Nancy: On my 35th birthday. Everything came to a screeching halt.

Joe: I was in the shower one day and I lost it. I was crying, thinking: Nancy's going to die—what am I going to do?! I literally could feel God, hear God, and He said, "You have to be strong. Get up."

Until then, I had been a passive Christian. I believed in God and believed in Christ, but I didn't read the Bible. We were going to church, but for me, it was on a very superficial level. I'd go, make my donation, and put it behind me until the next Sunday. I realized I needed God on a more-than-superficial level.

We put a stop to trying to get pregnant, per doctor's orders, and focused on Nancy. She had to have surgery. It went as well as it could go.

Nancy: After several good check-ups, we got the "go ahead" to try again, and right away I got pregnant. And then, right away, I miscarried.

Joe: Soon after that, we got referred to a specialist. I had poor numbers, and they discovered Nancy had a cyst.

Nancy: We both had to have surgery—two weeks apart. Then in June, we had a failed IUI. And in July, another failed IUI.

Joe: By this point, we were getting lots of body blows: Nancy having cancer, failed pregnancy, surgeries, failed IUI's. Then, my dad passed away....

I was at our lake house and I felt God, heard God, say to me, "Go on a dad trip." He was telling me to do this. I told Nancy, "I have to go to Vermont." We were in the middle of all these things and I said, "I have to go."

Nancy: I said, "Okay, go."

Joe: I did not have a good relationship with my father. I had to deal with that – and I never really had that moment with him before he died. So, I flew up to Vermont by myself, where he'd had a cabin that he'd go to with good friends.

I kept a journal of the trip. A diary. I had never felt closer to God than I did on that trip. I came back with peace about it. That's when my friend said, "You seem lighter."

In my mind, I was thinking, how could that possibly be? Because we were still in the middle of getting bad news after bad news after bad news... and nothing seemed to be working out like we'd hoped. Or planned.

Nancy: We had started coming to the infertility Bible study...

Joe: ... and being with other men in the group—seeing them go through things at the same time I was—that was great. It was the first place, outside our family, that I had spoken about Nancy's cancer. And, the group really helped open our minds to IVF because we heard so many other couple's stories.

Nancy: We learned more about doctors, and the procedure, and experiences people had had with IVF. It made us feel a lot more comfortable. I'd say we never struggled spiritually with whether to do it—it was whether we could afford it, whether we wanted to go this route.

That summer, before IVF, we started thinking about adoption, too. We talked about pursuing them both.

Joe: We had this crazy plan. We'd adopt, and by the time we had our IVF baby, we'd have two kids and be done.

We were planning—even though it wasn't our plan to make. You'd think that after all the struggles, we'd admit that we weren't in control. But instead, we just came up with more elaborate plans.

Nancy: Things went well with IVF. We had three embryos transferred just before Thanksgiving. We couldn't find out the results on Thanksgiving Day because no one was in the office, so we had to wait until the following week for blood work. During that time, my dad was diagnosed with cancer.

When we got the blood test results, it was positive and we told him we were pregnant. We thought he needed good news.

Joe: It was good news for him. He was very excited.

Nancy: Then, we had to call and tell him, "No, not anymore." That was hard. In August, just before the IVF, we'd talked with an attorney about adoption…

Joe: … and me being an attorney, I expected very good things. She was not good at all. In fact, we filed a complaint with the Bar. Even this person, who was supposed to be our partner in the journey, let us down.

Nancy: That was a tough time for us because everybody else in the class was getting pregnant.

Joe: Here we were, rejects of society because of not being able to conceive. We found a group of people all having the same problem. Then, Wilson and Sarah announced, "We're pregnant with twins." That was it; we were the last ones.

I looked at Nancy like, "*AAAGGGHHH*! What can we do? What can we possibly do?!"

Nancy: It was like, "What did we do to deserve this?"

Joe: You'd like to think that you get immune to that kind of thinking. But I wasn't.

Nancy: We were very angry after the failed IVF. The salt in the wound was the positive pregnancy test. And you just think, what else can we do? What have we done that's so wrong? Why, God?

Joe: You definitely go through that. Some days, you're totally in tune with God. You say, "Thank you for all my blessings."

And then other days, it's like, "You're not doing me right, God. This just isn't right. What did we do to deserve this?" It's not one constant feeling throughout the process.

Nancy: It's a roller coaster.

Joe: It's totally a roller coaster from hour-to-hour, and doctor phone call to doctor phone call.

Nancy: I remember going in for the consult after our failed IVF. We spoke with a therapist to make sure what we were feeling was normal—that we weren't losing it completely.

Joe: The therapist's single bit of advice was: do not make any big decisions in your state of mind. You know what we did with that advice? Completely ignored it. We mailed our check to the adoption consultant that day.

And I tell you, she literally called us two days later. We hadn't done anything but send a check and a profile. She called and said, "There's a baby girl born three months ago in Texas, and she's yours if you want her."

We said, "Whoa, whoa, whoa. We can't…. No, not so fast. Not yet."

Nancy: It was a pulse check.

Joe: We literally turned down several opportunities…

Nancy: … because she freaked us out! The first call was "Here's a 3-month-old and you can go get her tomorrow." Then, we got another call to show our profile in Utah. After we sent it, we felt we should wait. The gravity of the situation hit us hard.

But then, before we told the consultant not to ask us about any more, we got a third call about an opportunity in Florida.

Joe: It was, "There's a baby boy due on Christmas Day," which was less than 10 days away. "The original adoptive parents have backed out and the birth mother is looking for new profiles. Do you want us to send her yours?"

Something stirred in us and we said, "Yes" even though we thought, No way—we haven't done a home study or anything that the law requires to adopt. We totally had no expectations. All we had was a pretty profile.

Nancy: The consultant called the next day to say, "The birth mother has narrowed it down to two couples, and you're one of them."

Joe: She said, "You ought to talk to her." So, we did. The next night, we talked to her by phone—and it went well.

Nancy: Except that she wanted a Hindu family. Our profile says we're Christians. Still, she wanted to meet us. She was due in six days and at this point, we didn't even have a home study done.

Joe: So, we hired this amazing woman. We told her about our situation and—without blinking an eye—she said, "We can get this done." She got us through all the paperwork. There were roadblocks, but we got through them all.

Nancy: It usually takes people months to get home studies done; we got it done in two days. So, Saturday, which was December 20th…

Joe: … we said, "Goodbye family. We're going to meet the birth mother and maybe bring home a kid. We'll see."

Nancy: We drove to Florida and met her. She told us she was raised Catholic. She got married when she was 19, just to get out of the house. She had three kids right away. She turned her back on God because religion had been a bad experience for her.

Recently, she'd turned to Hinduism. The father of the baby was from SriLanka. The first family she'd chosen to adopt her baby was half-Hindu. They'd gone to doctor's appointments with her and talked quite a bit on the phone. But apparently, the potential adoptive mother was not very nice. She thought of the birth mother as "a vessel" to carry a child—not as a person whose feelings mattered.

The birth mother wanted a certain picture of a family, but then she got to know them and realized what mattered was who they were, not just what they looked like. She started to question her choice... and then, they made it easy for her by backing out.

Joe: That's what opened the door for us.

Nancy: We met her over dinner. It was surreal. Like a blind date. We talked about our story, our family, likes and dislikes. And after the meal, she said, "I want you to parent my child." So here it was, not even a week of knowing her, and she told us, "I want you to parent my child."

It was a happy moment, but also a scary moment; she could always change her mind. The earliest she could sign away her rights was two days after the baby was born. Some birth mothers change their minds once they meet the baby.

The next morning, she had a doctor's appointment and invited us to go hear the heartbeat. That was another surreal, weird situation. We all crowded into a little-bitty room....

Joe: That night, we took her and her two daughters out to dinner. It was Christmas Eve.

Nancy: It was all about her at that point. Making sure she was making the right decision for her and her family. If she wanted us, we would be there for her.

Joe: You could imagine a situation where you'd be trying to sell yourselves, but we were trying to put ourselves in her shoes. We would *never* have been able to do that—except that we'd gone through the class and heard so many stories about other adoptions. We knew that there was another side to this story.

Nancy: When people call me about adoption, the one thing I tell them is, "Love that birth mother. She is potentially going to give you the best gift ever. But, she's going through an incredibly hard time. She's making the best decision she can and it's completely out of love for that child. You've got to respect that and understand where she's coming from."

It's amazing that so many people respond, "I've never thought about it like that." Even Christians. It's amazing how that changes the process because it's not just Me-Me-Me, and Woe-Is-Me, and Look-At-All-I've-Been-Through....

Now, here's this woman—or couple—making a *huge* sacrifice. You change the focus and the waiting isn't as hard. You're more focused on witnessing through kindness, and just loving them. That's what the birth mother kept telling us, 'You're so nice. This feels so right."

Joe: When we drove down, we talked about it and agreed, we'd rather her not pick us than not be honest and up-front with our faith. If that kept her from picking us, then it wasn't meant to be.

That night at dinner, we were very direct in telling her, "He's going to be raised Christian." We knew this was serious and we needed to be genuine about who we are.

Nancy: God was with us. She told us later that she'd wanted her son to have a father and she knew she couldn't give him that. After meeting with us, it hit her that her son had always had a father, and that was God. That took a great weight off.

Joe: Christmas Day, the baby was due. We were thinking, Wow... there's going to be a baby born today and, in theory, he's going to be ours. But, he didn't come. The next day, we were thinking, today is going to be the day. Here he comes. But, no.

I honestly think that was God's handiwork because we needed those two days to get mentally and emotionally prepared. The night of the 26th, one of us said to the other, "We're ready now." And at 5am, we got a call from the birth mother saying her water broke. We drove over to the hospital. He came like a bullet—she had no drugs, all natural.

Nancy: We heard his first cries. We were right there. She put him in my arms. Two days later, she signed the papers before she was discharged. That was kind of bittersweet because we were hurting for her while we were getting the best gift ever.

We all walked out of the hospital together and she put him in the carseat. We hugged and, as we drove away, I heard the most sorrowful cry. It made my heart hurt. It was hard to be so happy when someone was hurting so much.

Joe: She recently wrote her story as part of the grieving process. She shared it with us this past week. What struck me was how close she came to having an abortion. She had set the appointment, she was going the next day, she woke up that morning and something inside of her made her change her mind. Instead of going to get an abortion, she shared what was going on with her family and decided to have the baby, despite pressure from the birth father to get an abortion.

I read that and realized how very, very close we were to not having our son. That was pretty scary.

Nancy: She also talked in her story about coming back to God, thanks to this experience. It didn't end with our visit.

Joe: It's never safe to presume you know God's plan, but if that *was* His plan—to make her believe in Him and in Christ—then it was a pretty good plan. It worked.

What did you learn through this infertility journey?

Nancy: I think when you're in it, no matter what anybody tells you, it's hard to find patience. You will get there, but you have to persevere—and that's hard.

Also, keep the lines of communication open... because it's a rollercoaster. We definitely grew closer through our journey.

Joe: First, I would say, take your problems to God and just unload on Him.

Second, take your problems to other people and talk about them. If you have a Bible study or small group at church, great. If not, share it with somebody you trust and whose insight and advice you value.

And third, know that it's definitely going to end. At some point in time, you will get through it. And, at the end of it, if all that happens is that you become closer to God, it's worth it.

Nancy: God's plan worked out much better than ours.

Redirecting Thoughts

In the beginning, our thoughts about the struggle with infertility are anxious and self-focused: When will it happen *for me*? What is causing this to happen *to me*? Why is everyone able to get pregnant, *but me*?

In response to these thoughts, we experience feelings, speak words and choose actions that reveal self-absorption and fearfulness. Why? Because our thoughts determine our feelings, words and actions. They are the catalyst. Whether we push for control, lash out in anger, or cower in the face of growing fear, we do it with minds, hearts and feet squarely in the Kingdom of Me.

By choice? We don't think so.

But, once we make the choice to put ourselves squarely in the Kingdom of God—and realize we have done so—we prove to ourselves there is an alternative to constant worry. We've discovered we don't have to think the thoughts we used to about infertility—thoughts of helplessness and hopelessness.

Now, we can claim and begin to see God at work, in and through our circumstances. We can be confident that there is a purpose for what we are experiencing. And even if we cannot foresee the exact outcome of this experience, we can anticipate "hope and a future," and claim victory-in-the-works.

Knowing that, we can finally find peace in the uncertainty of Now.

* * *

Pause and consider.... What has your experience been with "peace in the uncertainty of Now"? Have you *ever* experienced it? What were the circumstances? If it has not been a constant for you, why is that?

* * *

Does finding peace in the uncertainty of Now mean that we just wait? No.

This period of waiting in faithful anticipation is not intended to be wasted time. It serves an important purpose. We are to do more than just wait while God does the work; we are called to **active waiting**. That means we are to immerse ourselves in God's word, in order to make our minds more like that of Jesus—to see as he sees, and to choose as he would choose. In so doing, we give ourselves over to God's process of transformation.

The Bible advises, "Do not conform any longer to the pattern of this world, but be transformed by the renewing of your mind" [Romans 12:2]. This is our responsibility—and our opportunity—as citizens of the Kingdom of God. It is also the formula for transformation. When we fulfill this responsibility (by taking advantage of this opportunity), the renewing of our minds transforms our thoughts. We begin to see with eyes of faith, and to find peace in the will of God.

> The renewing of our minds begins to alter our experience

The apostle Paul writes," Don't shuffle along, eyes to the ground, absorbed with the things right in front of you. Look up, and be alert to what is going on around Christ.... *See things from his perspective*" [Colossians 3:2, Message, italics added]. That is spectacularly difficult in the midst of an infertility battle!

In the beginning, it would have been impossible for any

of us. But, the renewing of our minds actually transforms our thoughts, which begins to alter our experience. What seemed impossible no longer seems so; now, all things are possible [Mark 9:23].

So, how does this renewal occur? What changes in us?

Behavioral scientists tell us that our thoughts drive our feelings, words and actions. It follows that when our thoughts change, that alters not only what we feel, but also what we see, and say, and do. That, in turn, affects how others respond to us. All together, that affects our reality—and what we perceive as possible.

By renewing our minds, we don't decide to change our own thoughts and then will ourselves to do it. Our own limitations make that virtually impossible. Instead, we invite God to change our thoughts, redirect our emotions, and channel our words and actions in accordance with His plan for us. In other words, we consciously submit to His authority, wisdom and love for us. In so doing, we swing open the door to possibilities that otherwise would not enter our lives.

We are made strong and resilient by faith—restored to our better, truer selves by the work of the Holy Spirit. We are changed from within and prepared for what's coming. It is our intentional participation in this process that is active waiting.

●　　●　　●

Pause and consider.... Do you think "active waiting" is a solo pursuit, or a partnership with God? How does that make you feel? Have you tried active waiting as part of your infertility experience? With what results?

●　　●　　●

Consider what the psalmist writes, "Your word is a lamp to guide my feet and a light for my path" [Psalm 119:105, NLT]. By this, he means that God guides us when He speaks to us. Not only do our thoughts increasingly align with His will, as our minds are renewed; God also makes visible the path to "hope and a future." He enables us to see, with eyes of faith, what might otherwise be invisible to us.

"Guide my steps by your word," the psalmist continues [Psalm 119:133, NLT]. This request can become our prayer during this time of active waiting:

"Keep me on the right path, Lord. Help me trust you and what I am able to see only through eyes of faith. Through those eyes, enable me to see where you want me to go, what you want me to do, and whom you want me to trust. Guide my steps and my thoughts. Help me see that you are already at work in my life, preparing the way for a miracle."

To renew our minds, we will need to lean into the words of the Bible, actively seeking to receive God's messages for each of us. When we sincerely seek Him, we will find Him here— speaking directly to us, by the power of the Holy Spirit.

How will we find the right places to look? Where are the passages that will result in both "the renewing of your mind" and a greater peace in the midst of infertility? The rest of our discussions tackle these questions as we seek to find God's answers.

●   ●   ●

Pause and consider.... What kinds of thoughts does God want you to be thinking about infertility? Would they be substantially different from the ones that seem to bubble up on their own? Why are the thoughts that come naturally so often negative? Are they the only "realistic" ones to be thinking? Who has told you so—and why?

●   ●   ●

What kinds of thoughts does God want you to be thinking about infertility? Asking couples that question can bring on feelings of guilt, anger or grief when we are just beginning the Bible study. But now, well into our journey together, couples are mostly uncertain. What kinds of thoughts make sense to be thinking? How can anyone know? And, does it really matter?

Let's answer the last question first. *Yes, it matters.*

When our thoughts change, our actions follow. When our thoughts begin to follow a new trajectory—directed away from self, and toward God—our actions change to follow that same trajectory, as do our words and feelings. Instead of being fear-based, they become increasingly trust-based—based on the confident assurance that God is at work realizing the hope He has placed in each of our hearts.

This is not an overnight change. Even when most thoughts begin to shift from one direction to the other—from self, toward God—the renewal of our minds does not insure constant protection from persistent thoughts of helplessness or hopelessness. We are influenced less by impulse and anxiety. But still, the Bible advises, "...take captive *every* thought to make it obedient to Christ" [2 Corinthians 10:5, italics added].

• • •

You must take captive every helpless or hopeless thought

• • •

Take captive? Make obedient? These words conjure images of power struggles and conflict. That's appropriate because there is a spiritual battle going on within you. Anxiety and fearfulness give Satan an opening to fill your mind with lies and mistrust. He is, scripture reminds us, "the accuser" who exploits any opportunity to burden us with guilt, undermine our faith, and confuse us with doubt [Revelation 12:10].

But, "the bright light of Christ makes your way plain" [Ephesians 5:8, Message]. That's the promise: there is a way through. We must take an *active role* in keeping our thoughts aligned with their new trajectory—toward God, like the mind of Christ—in order to keep our feet on that path.

Which brings us back to the question: How do you renew your mind and redirect your thoughts? With what Bible verses? And what kinds of thoughts will you then start thinking?

The first answer comes from a story we have already studied: the disciples' encounter with a blind man. Do you remember how Jesus turned their question inside-out to infuse it with grace? Instead of punishment or condemnation, he showed them that the man's blindness simply set the stage for a miracle.

When you read more of the Bible, you notice that reality in the Kingdom of God is consistently like this—upside-down and insight-out, as compared to the expectations of the "real world." As you meditate on this truth, the implications begin to permeate your thinking, which begins to transform your thoughts about your infertility experience.

* * *

Invert your thoughts to see your experience from God's perspective

* * *

The trajectory of your thoughts begins to shift, away from self and toward God, as your mind applies this principle of inversion to your own experience. This change is you undergoing transformation.

You find yourself thinking new, different thoughts. Instead of rehearsing the thought, "infertility is a curse," you invert it and see the possibility of a pending miracle, through eyes of faith.

Rather than thinking "infertility is a dead-end," you choose to invert that thought and remember, God makes a way where there is no way.

Rather than seeing yourself as an emotional puddle, you invert the thought and see that you have become malleable. This is a blessing because it enables God to shape you into the parent He intends for you to be.

Instead of dwelling on yourself as out-of-control, you invert the thought and think of yourself as increasingly God-reliant. When you look at your experience this way, you can actually see the advantage in losing (the illusion of) control.

Rather than lost, you begin to think of yourself as a seeker, actively attempting to find the Way. Rather than lonely, you think of yourself as longing for, and looking expectantly for, God's company. Instead of dwelling on "I want a baby... now!" you chose to keep thinking, "God knows what I need, and when." Instead of telling yourself, "I should keep worrying and trying to control this process," you choose to think, "thank you, God, for peace that passes understanding. I believe You are in control."

●   ●   ●

Pause and consider.... Do these examples of "inverted thinking" give you a new perspective on your infertility experience? Are you willing to trade the illusion of control for this new way of seeing things?

●   ●   ●

To be clear, the principle of inversion thinking is not wishful thinking. It is the renewing of your mind. It is you taking captive thoughts that are not from God. It's not hoping that the truth isn't true, and just whistling in the dark. It is Bible-based, God-blessed thinking that relies on the promises of God to His children.

Here are many more examples that will help transform your thinking and renew your mind. Use these promises of scripture to strengthen your hope:

❖ When you confess, "I'm afraid," God reassures you, **I have not given you a spirit of fear** [II Timothy 1:7].

❖ When you stress, "I'm always worried," Jesus urges, **Cast all your cares on me, because I care for you** [I Peter 5:7].

❖ When you despair, "I don't know what to think," God says, **Count on me to give you wisdom through Christ** [I Corinthians 1:30].

❖ When you wonder, "What if it's impossible?" Jesus says, **What is impossible with men is possible with God** [Luke 18:27].

❖ When you can't figure out, "What now?" God says, **I will direct your steps** [Proverbs 3:5,6].

❖ When you sense, "We're both exhausted," Jesus says, I **will give you rest** [Matthew 11:28].

❖ When you are tempted to think, "I am so alone in this," God promises, **I will never abandon you** [Hebrews 13:5].

❖ When you worry, "We're running out of patience, money, stamina, options,…and hope," God promises, **I will meet all your needs.** [Philippians 4:19].

❖ When you despair, "It's not worth it," God assures you, **It will be worth it** [Romans 8:28].

❖ When you are tempted to think, "I can't do this anymore," the Bible promises, **You can do all things through Christ who strengthens you** [Philippians 4:13].

❖ When you wonder, "How will I survive this?" God says, **My grace is sufficient for you** [II Corinthians 12:9].

●   ●   ●

Pause and consider…. Which of these promises speak to you? How can you keep them top-of-mind in the weeks ahead?

●   ●   ●

When you consciously and intentionally apply the principle of inversion thinking in order to take fearful thoughts captive, you redirect your thinking in God's direction. Because you know God's word is "a lamp to your feet and a light to your path," you can be confident that it shows you the way—through infertility, to the blessing of parenthood that awaits you.

When a thought comes to mind, consider it from the Kingdom-of-God perspective. Is it infused with grace? Full of trust? Does it steer you toward feelings, words and actions that reflect your faithful citizenship in the Kingdom? Or, is this a thought to be taken captive, and inverted?

• • •

Learn to discern the source of your thoughts

• • •

With practice, you will find you are increasingly able to discern the difference. The Holy Spirit will give you the gift of discernment to use in just this way, for just this purpose. As you do, you will undergo the transformation that occurs when your mind is renewed by God's truth, and your life is lived with confidence in His perfect plan.

As David writes, "Teach me your ways, O Lord, and I will walk in your truth; Give me an undivided heart... For great is your love toward me..." [Psalm 86:11-13].

What kinds of thoughts does God want us to be thinking about infertility? We have just considered a number of compelling possibilities. Now, consider what one member of our group said when she was ready to connect several ideas and share her insights with us.

"I feel like I'm slowly lifting my head and expanding my view of this experience. Instead of seeing myself as the star in my own drama, now I see that this is *God's* story—unfolding in *my* life. Hitting the wall made me reach for God. And somehow, reaching out to Him has made more room for Him in my life. And in this infertility experience, too."

She concluded, "I think those are things God wants me

to be thinking about."

Yes, indeed He does. A single step of faith sets many things in motion—most of which, we do not see except in hindsight.

So, as we continue to step out in faith, where do we go? This Bible verse gives us direction:

"Although the Lord gives you the bread of adversity and the water of affliction, your teachers will be hidden no more; with your own eyes you will see them. Whether you turn to the right or to the left, your ears will hear a voice behind you, saying, 'This is the way; walk in it.'"

Isaiah 30:20-21

What a promise this is for people who are suffering and feeling lost! We are told that, despite our experience of suffering (which God has allowed to enter into our lives), we are not abandoned or alone. We will see clearly who can help us to understand. We will hear clearly a voice that knows the way. And, we will find the path—because we will be led to it.

What does this mean to a roomful of infertile couples? And what does it say to you? It says that you can't see around the corner, but God already knows what's coming. He knows every twist and turn in the path your life will take. So, as He looks down that path, He sees what you need now... to be who you'll need to be then.

What you need now might be difficult challenges, or specific opportunities, or experiences that strengthen your relationship with Him. If so, He will bring those into your life in order to lay a firm foundation for the future.

He will also send teachers who can help you recognize these experiences as the well-disguised blessings that they are. This book is one of those teachers for you.

Who you'll need to be then—sometime in the future—is known only to God. You will be the ideal parent for the specific soul(s) He intends to entrust to you. It won't be a random, accidental match or a slapped-together solution. You will be the perfectly-chosen parent for that particular child. It will literally be a match made in heaven.

In your role as parent, you will need to be a confident leader, an attentive guardian, a trustworthy steward, and a gentle, loving shepherd. You will personify the love of God in the life of a child. So right now, God is working in your life to equip you to be all those things—and more— when the time comes.

> • • •
>
> You will personify the love of God in the life of a child
>
> • • •

Do you feel you are already equipped? Is your impatience based, in part, on your sense that you could not be more prepared? You will need to trust that God knows whether you are ready for the life He intends for you and for this child.

And, that time *will* come. Soon enough for you? It doesn't feel that way. At the perfect time, in hindsight? Yes, absolutely.

The Bible promises us, "What is impossible for people is possible with God" [Luke 18:27, NLT]. We need to claim that promise and very intentionally let go of our anxious questions— *when, and how*?!—trusting that God knows.

With confidence built on a foundation of trust, we can claim the promise that "all things are possible," and turn our attention to becoming the stewards God intends us to be for the next generation.

Reflections

_____
_____
_____
_____
_____
_____
_____
_____
_____
_____
_____
_____
_____
_____
_____
_____
_____
_____
_____
_____
_____
_____
_____

Toni & Mike

How did your story begin?

Toni: We met later in life and got married late…

Mike: … I was 39 and she was 34.

Toni: We knew we wanted a family, but we didn't jump right into it because we wanted to enjoy being newlyweds. By the time we started, the OB/GYN said, "You need to see a specialist." She referred me right away.

Mike: Her OB/GYN told her, "Thirty-five is a crucial age."

Toni: Going in, I had reservations about using science to get pregnant. I felt like—if it was supposed to happen, it would happen naturally—and God would answer my prayers.

Mike: I'm in healthcare, so I took a more scientific view of this stuff. We were older, so you've got to look at the statistics on that.

Toni: When we talked to the doctor about the statistics, we realized we'd better try to do something or it might be too late to do anything. So, we did an IUI. It was unsuccessful. During the process, I developed some cysts in response to the Letrozole. I took that as a sign. If I hadn't taken the medicine, I wouldn't have gotten the cysts.

We decided to take a year off. We just kind of backed away from the whole thing. Something just didn't feel right about it.

Mike: That year off, we thought we'd get pregnant.

Toni: We tried, but it didn't work. So then, we said, "Let's try IUI again" and went through three more. All three IUI's failed. The next step was IVF.

Mike: As far as the science of IVF, that was not a problem for me...

Toni: ... but I was struggling with the whole faith-science thing. It was such a heavy burden. I'm a person who doesn't like medicine, doesn't like needles. To have to do all that seemed to go against everything I believe. I was praying that God would make it happen without all that.

Fortunately, we met with a Christian counselor. He made a strong point that stuck with me and really turned out to be a good insight. He said, "Maybe God is working through the doctor, instead of working through you."

Mike: Meanwhile, I learned about infertility and about how many people struggle. I learned that with IVF, you can find out where your problems are. How many eggs do you make? Does the egg fertilize? Is that a problem? Does it stay attached to you? There are things they can figure out. That's the science aspect, and I thought that was good.

Toni: We talked about doing IVF and decided to start the process.

Mike: The first time we tried it, they said we didn't have enough eggs. So, they cancelled the cycle. They didn't even do a retrieval.

Toni: About that time, we saw a note in the church bulletin about the infertile couples' class. We had already started our journey, but we still didn't know what was ahead of us and if there was the possibility of getting pregnant. So, the class came at a good point. We started going and started praying more.

The second IVF, they thought there were two or three eggs to get. The doctor was looking at the statistics, my age, and the number of eggs we had—and it wasn't looking good. She said, "We'll go through with this if you want to," but she thought it was very unlikely to work. Doctors go by statistics.

I said, "If there's something in there, let's go get it."

Then, the doctor told me, "You may want to consider adoption." Before even trying the IVF, she was already expecting a negative outcome!

I remember saying, "I know you can only do what you can do, but there's another factor involved here." I didn't want to say, "God is doing the work" because I didn't want to offend her, but that's what I was thinking.

Mike: We decided to do the IVF.

Toni: When we came out of recovery, I asked, "How many eggs did we get?" She said, "One." I said, "We got one!" Everyone got real quiet because they were thinking, that's not good.

Mike: But it fertilized, and they put it back in. Statistically, it was not likely to work. But, it worked for us. That became our son.

Toni: We had *one* egg, and then it fertilized, and then we got pregnant. Everything was normal; everything went great. The doctor kept saying to us, "You don't realize how lucky you are!"

She started using our story in counseling sessions with other couples as an example of what's possible. I'd go into the office and the nurses would say, "You are the poster child for infertility. The one-egg wonder! Do you realize, this never happens?!" I kept that in the back of my mind.

Then, a year later, I showed up at her office and she was so surprised to me. She said, "Do you know how lucky you were to get pregnant the first time? And now you're back?"

I was more confident than the doctor was. I had the confidence from God because I'd prayed and prayed. We'd gone through the class, I'd started going to the fertility prayer group, and I felt full of faith. Instead of thinking, "why me?" I had started thinking, "why *not* me?" I felt confident because I was asking God to make it happen for us.

I said, "I know you're talking statistically. But, tell me if you want to work with me on this—because if you don't, I'll go to another physician. I don't want someone looking at my chart and snickering when I come in, thinking, how does she think she's going to get pregnant when she's got these numbers? I need to know that you're in this with me. If you're not, I'm not in the right clinic."

I was so positive; I didn't let her bring me down. She said there was a new IVF protocol that she'd consider trying with us. That's what we did.

We got five eggs. When she told us, we said, "That's five versus one before, and that's great." But she was still downplaying it. She said, "You know, the quality on all of these is not that great. I want to put them all back in."

We were like, "Five?! You want to put five back in?!" We were just praying that we didn't end up with triplets or something crazy like that.

She said, "Do you know how lucky you would be just to get one?"

Mike: We went back and had a positive pregnancy test.

Toni: Then, we went in for the ultrasound. She wasn't getting a strong heartbeat. She and the nurse were huddled together talking. I said, "I feel pregnant. I *feel* pregnant."

The doctor said, "We'd expect you to have a little bit stronger heartbeat." In the back of my mind, I knew she was thinking—This isn't good.

I just looked at her and said, "You know what? I think it's just early." I stayed strong in my faith. When I went back two weeks later, I told them, "I feel pregnant!"

The doctor said, "Well, let's see." We went in for the ultrasound and there was a strong heartbeat. Everything looked great. It all went great—and then, our second son was born.

How did the infertility Bible study help you?

Toni: We have been blessed with so many things in our lives that I almost felt guilty asking God for help. I had to learn how to pray about this because I'd always just prayed "thank you" for everything. I remember I talked a little bit about that in one of the classes. The leader said, "There's nothing wrong with asking. In fact, God tells us to ask Him."

The class also helped me get more familiar with the Bible. Where were the scriptures that could be relevant to me? How to pray, why to pray…. Once I had all that going for me, I just felt really confident.

Mike: One thing from the class that helped me was realizing you may have to use science or you may have to adopt, but there *is* a way to have a child. It may not be the way that you thought it was going to happen, but if you want to have a child, you can have one. That gave people hope.

Toni: It was helpful that Mike was supporting me by going to the class. When we'd come home, we'd talk about other people's stories and about supporting each other. That did make it easier.

When we first started with the class, I remember seeing a woman I recognized at the park on Sunday afternoon. She called out, "Hey! You were in our class this morning." And I thought, I don't want to be in the Club of Infertile Women. But as more

time went by, I went through the class and the prayer group—
and now, I feel like I'm a spokesperson for the whole thing. I
have no problem sharing our story or trying to encourage others.
Now, it comes so easily.

What did you learn from your infertility journey?

Toni: Infertility is an emotional roller coaster. I stuck with my
faith and kept praying, asking God to help me get through it.
Any time I started to feel weakness around my faith or started
getting stressed, I'd try to read something positive, or come to
the class, or go to the prayer group. I leaned on God *a lot*.

When we were waiting for IVF results, people said I was
so calm. I said, "You know what? I've done everything I can do.
The doctors have done what they can do. Now it's up to God."

I talk to women who are older and trying to get pregnant.
Often, their doctors haven't given them a lot of hope—or they've
thrown a lot of statistics at them. I tell them putting their faith in
God, instead of in those numbers, may get them where they need
to be. Don't let the statistics tell your story. If it's in your heart
and you pray, it will happen.

Mike: I guess you don't think about infertility until you start
trying to have kids. As a guy, I'm more sensitive now about saying things to friends.

Toni: This experience makes you more sensitive. It's made me
open up and talk about it. If we'd gotten pregnant on IUI, I
wouldn't still be going to the prayer group. But, I do it because I
want to inspire someone who might be sitting on the fence thinking, "Is science the way to go, or should I keep praying and
trying naturally?"

Maybe, if I pass on the comment the counselor made to
me, it'll help someone else make their decision with more peace.

Waiting & Anticipating

When the Bible tells us, "Do not conform any longer to the pattern of this world, but be transformed by the renewing of your mind," it reveals what God wants for us: complete transformation. The Bible makes clear that this transformation is for our benefit. It also benefits the Kingdom of God.

Even so, because we have the freedom to choose, we can elect to respond with gratitude, indifference, or hostility. God will not force our hand, although He may allow circumstances to make the choice clear to us.

If and when we choose to follow Him, we agree to be transformed. We submit ourselves to His authority—inviting His will to guide our steps, and His word to be a light for our path. For some people, this submission is only a superficial, situation-specific transformation. A temporary fix. When circumstances return to "normal," unfortunately, so do they.

But, we are called to participate in a lasting transformation. That is part of the purpose for this time of active waiting. God wants us to undergo a deeper, more profoundly life-changing transformation than we ever have before. Does that mean all this suffering is punishment? Coercion? Not at all. It's an invitation. This time of active waiting is a time of opportunity. A blessing-in-disguise.

To make the most of this opportunity, the Bible tells us that we will need to stop conforming to the pattern of this world and start participating in the renewing of our minds. That means we are to take all thoughts captive and make them obedient to Christ. Why to Christ? Because, as he told us, "I and the Father are one."

When we make our thoughts obedient to Christ, we align them with God's thoughts and His will. Our thoughts become God's thoughts *in us* and *through us*. Soon, we hear His voice speak *to us*. Before long, we see His path appear ahead of us. Ultimately, we know which way to go because His thoughts *are* our thoughts.

● ● ●

What thoughts fill your mind right now?

● ● ●

This is really about learning constant mindfulness. What is your mind full of right now? What is it full of when you move through your day? When you interact with your partner? When you see a pregnant woman or a new baby? When you have another period—or your spouse does? When someone offhandedly asks, "When are you two going to start a family?"

God wants your mind to be full of His promises. *That* will transform you... and your infertility experience. It will lighten the burden you currently bear, and prepare you for the blessings He has in store.

● ● ●

Pause and consider.... How does the concept of mindfulness help you understand the need to "take all thoughts captive"? How do you think it might relate to experiencing "peace that passes understanding"?

● ● ●

As the apostle Paul writes, "Every part of scripture is God-breathed and useful one way or another—showing us truth, exposing our rebellion, correcting our mistakes, training us to live God's way" [II Timothy 3:16, The Message].

The Bible is given to us as an instruction manual, to help lead us through the challenges of life. It contains all the wise counsel we need, from the One who knows us best. We should immerse ourselves in it because the promises and lessons it contains will transform us—*and* our experience.

During this time of active waiting, we have a chance to work with God—to confront our challenges, and to enable blessings to enter into our lives. How? By filling our minds and hearts with biblical truths about what is possible, and whom we can trust. The Bible teaches us that with God, all things are possible [Luke 18:27]. *With God.* We want that truth active and alive in our experience—the sooner, the better.

> We can work *with* God to bring blessings into our lives

Will filling our minds with thoughts like these bring on the blessings we want, when we want them? God doesn't make us that promise. And we already know we can't force our own timetable onto infertility. So, when do the blessings begin?

They already have.

The apostle Paul reassures us that "...the peace of God, which transcends all understanding, will guard your hearts and minds in Christ Jesus" [Philippians 4:7]. This is the greatest blessing possible—a peace that does not depend on what we experience, or when, but on whom we trust. That is the result of true transformation.

When we make room in our lives, and find time in our schedules, for the renewing of our minds, we make that transformation a priority. We lean into our understanding of God's purpose for this time of active waiting, and we say "yes" to becoming the people He intends for us to be. Often, an emphatic *"yes!"* accelerates the transformation—which can bring blessings into our lives that much sooner.

In our group, we had already seen one man changed by God. Remember Joe? His spontaneous testimony spoke volumes to the other men in that group.

Tempted to keep their pain hidden, their voices silent, and their stoicism firm, they saw the effect of true transformation firsthand. They saw the peace they wanted in their own lives. That man had found a way through the heartache and uncertainty of infertility—and they intended to follow the same path.

They followed his lead and began participating more actively in our group. Several of them also began attending the men's prayer breakfast. They even initiated a couples' dinner to further strengthen their connections and demonstrate their support for one another. They had not solved the problem of infertility, but they had found the path toward peace.

So, how can you find that same peace? How can you stop conforming to the world and begin the renewing of your mind that will transform you and your experience? We begin to answer that question by looking first at what the world offers infertile couples.

●   ●   ●

Pause and consider.... How would you compare what the world has offered *you*—in terms of comfort, understanding or meaningful support—to what you're finding in these lessons? How often does the world meet your deepest needs?

●   ●   ●

According to a recent *Newsweek* cover story, six million couples in the U.S. are currently struggling with infertility. That's one-in-every-six couples of childbearing age. Unfortunately, that reality collides head-on with the media mania over celebrity pregnancies, multiple births and mega-families.

It is impossible to buy groceries without seeing photogenic celebrities and their new babies' pictures splashed across glossy magazines. The stars' urges to share their baby stories are usually just thinly-veiled self-promotion. The same is often true of parents whose multiple multiples or mega-families bring them fifteen minutes of fame.

Their children enable them to bid for our attention: *Here's another reason for everyone to look at me!* Still, it's hard not to look and wonder, "What if that were me? What if I were pregnant, or holding my newborn? What if I had news to tell and photos to share?"

It's no coincidence that these two trends—infertility and expanding-family mania—are gaining momentum at the same speed. As infertility becomes an increasingly common problem for American couples, fertility success stories are increasingly marketable. Not surprisingly, the media continue to cover the stories that sell best.

Is there any harm in that?

Actually, yes. These success stories, and the contrived images that accompany them, can pour salt in the wound of infertility. They invite negative, self-pitying thoughts to enter the minds of infertile readers and viewers. Does that mean we should condemn these stories? Of course not. Does it mean we should avoid them? Maybe.

> Other people's success stories often pour salt in the wound of infertility

If they invoke thoughts like, *Why not me? Why her/him/them? I'm sure I'd be a better parent* (and so on), then they're not helpful. Thoughts like these are contrary to turning away from self, and toward God. They make it harder to resist the anxiety and despair that keep whispering: *Why is my story so tragic? Why am I never the happy one?*

Of course, media images aren't the only culprit. And the effect is not just on women. Both partners in an infertile couple often find that baby showers and other cultural celebrations of fertility have the same effect. Baby announcements, baby photos, baby stories, baby clothing, baby stores… baby everything!

All of it, cumulatively, seems to suggest that you are having a problem no one else is experiencing. That's a lie. But, it is a very seductive one. It isolates you—and it drives a wedge of despair between you and confident hope.

*   *   *

Pause and consider.... How often do you dwell on the lie that everyone else is having a baby, and you will never succeed? How does that affect your hopefulness? Do you see the connection between the thoughts that fill your mind and the strength of your hope?

*   *   *

Part of your role during this time of active waiting is to see through the lie and replace it with the Truth. This is what it means to lean into the process of transformation.

So, how do you replace a persistent lie with the Truth? You change what you feed your mind. You say "no" to the media messages that open the door to self-pity. Instead of those junk food, fantasy images, you give yourself spiritual nourishment. Food for the soul.

You say "no" to negative thoughts that arise when you get invited to another baby shower, get handed another baby photo, or get invited to feel another baby kick through another woman's belly. If need be, you say "no" to these invitations.

As you do this, you turn away from self-absorption while setting healthy boundaries that protect your vulnerable heart. You say "no" to self-pity, but "yes" to self-protection. That is good and appropriate self-care.

Another part of active waiting is making time to marinate in God's word—renewing your mind with His promises of faithfulness, peace, hope and a future. You need to seek out compassionate friends who understand the challenge of remaining faith-full during this journey. You need to ask God to lead you to new opportunities, and to create new possibilities. And then, you must trust Him to fill your mind and heart with hope.

Daily... hourly... minute-by-minute... you need to say "no" to the world's incessant invitations to be consumed with yourself. Instead, say "yes" to drawing nearer to God, and being transformed. By making this choice—*again and again*—you begin moving toward the promise, God will keep you in perfect peace [Isaiah 26:3].

The world's mantra, "it's all about me!" isn't God's truth. It is a seductive lie that opens the door to self-pity and self-absorption, which separate you from God.

So, if the world isn't offering you any sustenance during this time of waiting, what should you dwell on when you need food for the spirit—and the strength to keep hoping? What truths does God want you to be thinking about infertility? Thankfully, He offers a number of answers to this question.

• • •

What does God want you to be thinking about now?

• • •

Let's begin with the word "infertile." It is a word seared into your heart that separates you from all those who are able to conceive. It is a deeply painful word that is difficult to utter aloud, except to fellow sufferers. What if we invert it, and seek a grace-filled understanding of its deeper, metaphorical meaning?

The dictionary describes infertile as being like "fallow ground." What does fallow mean? It is defined several ways. First, as "cultivated land allowed to lie idle during the growing season."

The words "allowed to lie idle" suggest that the One who cultivates this land has made an intentional choice, for a specific purpose. "To lie idle" implies a period of resting or temporarily waiting, but *not* death or permanent stillness. "During the growing season" makes clear that, although other fields may be producing, it is better for this particular field to rest and be renewed now. The One who has cared for this field for many years knows it to be true.

How does this perspective reframe the way you see your

own infertility?

A second definition of fallow is the "tilling of land without sowing for a season." What is tilling? Tilling is "preparation with the intent to wait for the ideal time." The One who oversees the field is preparing it; He is doing so with the intention of waiting only until the perfect time. He knows both the field and the crop He intends to grow so well, that He can sense what will be most beneficial.

"Without sowing for a season" affirms the seed's need for the best possible soil to maximize its potential. The temptation to grow now is resisted by the One who knows waiting will bring a more bountiful harvest.

How does this perspective reframe the way you see your own infertility?

The concept of infertile or fallow ground is all about the choice to take a loss this season for greater gain the future. When we apply this understanding to the experience of infertility, we see that God's goal is to make use of a season of fallowing (infertility) to prepare the soil (you, the future parent) to help nourish and grow what is planted (the child/children God puts in your life).

❀   ❀   ❀

Pause and consider.... Does this version of the fallow field metaphor speak to your infertility experience? Re-read it and consider the question carefully. In what ways might God be tilling the soil of your life? How does this affect your willingness to wait "for the ideal time"?

❀   ❀   ❀

God wants the best for the next generation. So, He invests time and effort into this season of preparing *you*. The fallow field lies in wait, full of potential, anticipating the perfect season after a wisely planned period of preparation. The "seed" waits, too. It will not flourish without optimal conditions.

Without this critical step in the process, God cannot expect what is planted to reach its fullest potential—and that is His desire: to give the child who is destined to come into your life the best possible environment in which to grow and thrive.

The fallow field metaphor extends beyond the infertile body to include the mind, the heart and the spirit. God is at work in all parts of your life—weeding out the undesirable growth, turning things over, exposing what needs to be uncovered, allowing light and living water to reach what needs nourishment. He sees the infertile parts of your life, and He longs for them to be abundantly healthy.

The Bible says, "See how the farmer waits for the land to yield its valuable crop and how patient he is for the Autumn and Spring rains. You, too, be patient and stand firm..." [James 5:7-8].

Just as the farmer is the steward of the land, entrusted with responsibility for its abundance, God is the steward of your life—to the extent you'll allow Him to be.

He wants every part of your life to be abundantly fertile ground, consistently producing all the fruits of the spirit. These are visible signs of the vibrant life within you that emerge when you are connected to the source of life, which is God. They include love, joy, peace, patience, kindness, goodness, faithfulness, gentleness and self-control [Galatians 5:22].

> God longs for the infertile parts of your life to be abundantly healthy

Have you felt a need for these lately? God is at work in your life creating fertile ground for them to flourish.

Why, if God can do anything, can't your fertile field be ready overnight? Why must there be suffering involved in preparing for the future? There are several possible answers to these frustrating questions.

First, to extend the metaphor of the field, seasons must

be considered. Winter appears to be a season of death, when much of Nature seems utterly lifeless. But, we know from experience that Spring always follows. We trust that it will come, even when we don't see any evidence that it is coming. We know life will literally spring from what looks like dead ground when the time is right.

Similarly, a season of infertility looks like an unending period of dormancy and death. God wants us to trust that He is both able and willing to bring a season of renewal and life into our lives—in His perfect timing. The seed of hope He has planted in our hearts will survive this season of darkness, and it will carry us into the season of light. Can we wait with the same confident hope that tells us Spring will follow Winter?

◉　◉　◉

Pause and consider.... How do the concepts of fallow fields, seeds of hope, and seasons of darkness and light speak to you? Do these metaphors give you a deeper understanding of how God is at work in the midst of your infertility? Do they strengthen your hope or confidence? How so?

◉　◉　◉

This season of waiting may also involve pruning, as God changes and redirects our growth—toward His light, for greater fullness, cutting out unhealthy areas, rounding out thin patches, and strengthening our roots. Before we can sustain additional growth, He wants us to be completely healthy and ready ourselves. This is evidence of His wisdom, patience and care for us.

Jesus taught the disciples this same lesson, saying, "I am the true vine, and my Father is the gardener. He cuts off every branch in me that bears no fruit, while every branch that does bear fruit he prunes, so that it will be even more fruitful" [John 15:1-2].

Jesus makes a distinction between cutting off branches

that are essentially worthless, and pruning those that bear fruit in order to stimulate more abundant growth. In this time of active waiting, he teaches that God is working steadily—as the knowledgeable gardener—reshaping our lives to nurture stronger roots in faith. He is cutting off worthless branches, like self-absorption and self-pity, to facilitate more productive growth in all areas of our lives.

We must remember that this is for our benefit and the benefit of the Kingdom of God. It is for our growth as children of God, and as future stewards of God's children.

The Bible clearly states that "...you are God's field..." [I Corinthians 3:9]. It is God's desire that you understand what He is doing in that field, and why. Just as sun, water, and time enable the earth to bring forth a great bounty, the light of Christ, the grace of God, and the trials you are currently experiencing with infertility will bring a great harvest—in God's perfect timing.

That is the plan.

Will you wait for God to bring forth His very best? Not because you have to, but because you choose to? If you can say, "Yes, God, even when I don't understand fully, I will choose to trust your timing and purpose," you will delight Him. He, in turn, will delight in bringing forth a miraculous harvest result—above all that you could ask or imagine, according to His power at work within you [Ephesians 3:20].

Reflections

Cathi & Brent

How did your story begin?

Cathi: We dated all through college and got married a year after I graduated. I was 23 and Brent was about to turn 25.

Brent: We knew we wanted kids someday, but it wasn't a rush at all. My parents had kids in their early 30's. And I teach—and coach lacrosse—so I'm around kids all the time. Plus, I was getting my master's degree.

Cathi: We were very relaxed about it. My sister got married after us, and she started trying to have kids right away. She went through a lot with infertility. I didn't want to start trying until she succeeded. I didn't want to get pregnant on the first try and make her feel bad.

Now, I laugh to think it could have been that easy.

Brent: At Christmas, our Sunday school class went around the room and every couple said their goal for next year. Everyone in the room said, "We want to start a family. We want to start a family. We want to start a family. "

We weren't there yet, so we joined a different Sunday school class. Then, everybody in that class started having kids.

Cathi: [laughing] They blew by us.

Brent: We eventually stopped going to Sunday school about three months into trying to get pregnant. But we stayed involved with a small group. It's us and five other couples. We meet once a week. It's a group with very deep relationships.

Cathi: Still, we didn't share our infertility with them until about eight months into the journey.

Brent: Once a year, our small group would have each couple take a week to talk about the big issues in their lives. It just happened to be our turn when we hit a year of trying. We let them know what we were going through.

They're all our age, so they were there to help, but they didn't quite understand. None of them had gone through it. Some of them already had children.

Cathi: It was impossible to explain to them what infertility is like. Watching someone go through it is *nothing* like going through it yourself. I don't think anyone who hasn't been through it completely understands.

Brent: Meanwhile, we kept trying....

Cathi: The OB/Gyn came up with a game plan. First, take tests. Brent's came back fine. Mine did, too. Totally normal. In a way, that was good because there wasn't a problem. But in a way, it was disappointing because there wasn't a problem to fix.

The OB/Gyn said we'd just start with Clomid and go from there. Clomid made me crazy. I'd get so frustrated. And I had really strong feelings about random, stupid stuff.

Brent: I finally told my family. Nobody was expecting grandchildren yet—no one was really pushing for it.

But, I'd hear about it all the time from the kids I teach: "When are you gonna have kids? Why don't you have kids?" That was really awful, constantly having that brought up. Plus, I'd hear it from co-workers. I'm very open with the kids I coach and with my colleagues, but I couldn't tell them this wasn't a personal choice… "I want children, but we're having trouble."

Cathi: We had to come up with some pat answers, like, "At some point, God will bless us with children."

Brent: I'd usually say, "No kids yet. Not right now." It's just not something you discuss. It's not something you bring up— even with your best friends.

Cathi: We felt completely isolated. People wanted to be supportive, but they didn't know how. Plus, I was getting increasingly frustrated that the people in our small group started getting pregnant.

Brent: They were very worried about how we'd react.

Cathi: When they'd call—to invite us to dinner and break the news—I'd say to Brent, "They're totally pregnant."

I would walk into places looking for clues. I'd see so-and-so not drinking and think, she's definitely pregnant. I would try to prepare myself, so I wasn't caught off-guard. So I wouldn't have that look like, "I'm going to cry right now in front of everybody." It sounds ridiculous, but I couldn't be surprised because I wouldn't be able to keep it together.

Almost all the couples in our small group got pregnant while we were trying.

Brent: We were so happy for them, but so frustrated at the same time.

Cathi: When the first couple got pregnant, I was devastated. But it was their second child, so I thought, at least I won't have to go to a baby shower. That's how I got through it.

The next couple that got pregnant, it was their first child—so I had to do the baby shower. I really struggled with that. I had to ask myself, "Do I think I can go and not make a scene? Do I think I can keep it together?" I did end up going, but I had to really pray about it. And then, I had to power through it.

Brent: Normally, it wouldn't have been unusual for us to go visit people from our small group in the hospital. You'd think a new baby would be a great reason to go. But during infertility, we never went there. We couldn't.

Cathi: Especially with them all getting pregnant. Every week, I'd see their bigger bellies. The way I dealt with it was I'd go buy some cute little gift. That was my outlet… I'd get to go look at cute little baby things. Even though they weren't for me, I could go and give it to them later. It was important to do something, versus not acknowledging it.

Brent: Spring had been bad, but by the Fall, I was teaching on autopilot. I was doing what I had to do, but I was not focusing. I couldn't. I was so distracted. There was nothing I could do about it.

Cathi: Normally, we're not those kind of people at all. We would never phone it in and be less than 100% overachieving, perfectionist people—but infertility kicks your butt. That's just the way it is.

Meanwhile, everybody we knew was getting pregnant. Everybody! Everywhere we went. Everyone was pregnant.

And then you joined the infertility Bible study?

Cathi: We came to the class just as we were about to embark on the whole reproductive endocrinologist thing.

Brent: We'd been looking for something like this at other churches. We were so frustrated, we had to find something. I was looking at every church I could find… but nothing. And then, this group finally started.

We were really ready to meet other couples who'd been

through this.

Cathi: There was hope in hearing other people's stories, but also, I thought: this could be way worse than I ever imagined. Some of the stories... people with late miscarriages, cancer, other things that happened... I was like, that is so much stuff to have going on! Some people had done tons of IUI's, IVF's....

Brent: But we started to see, as we went through the process, that we could totally imagine doing all that. Until I was in the process, I'd look at it from the outside and think, no way would I do three IVF's. But by the time we got there, I was thinking, there's no way I'd do less than three IVF's—if that's what it takes.

Cathi: Your perception of what you're willing to do totally changes along the way. I'm terrified of needles, but I realized I could survive. You tell yourself, "I can do this one more thing." And you think, what if I don't do this and it could be the thing that would've worked?

Brent: We got into all this reproductive endocrinology and I thought, we'll always regret it if we don't try this. And I was surprised by that. It's not what I would have expected at all.

Cathi: When we got to talk to other couples, it was great to talk to somebody who totally got what you were going through. That helped a lot.

Brent: At first, we wondered if the class was going to be what we needed because there were so many couples who'd gone through it already and gotten to the other side. Was this going to help us?

But then, we'd break into small groups and talk with those couples.... They'd listen and you could tell they understood. They wanted to hear what we had to say, and then they'd say, "We've been there." I didn't realize it would feel so helpful to hear that. Sometimes, they'd say, "We've been there—and worse."

Cathi: But they still believed in God!

Brent: During this time, I felt very questioning in my faith. A minister asked me, "What will happen to your faith if you two don't get pregnant?" That question was really useful to think about, but I was really scared about how I'd answer it.

There was such a desire to have a family and be a father … what if it didn't happen? I didn't know what my faith would look like if I couldn't get there. I didn't want the answer to be that my faith would be shattered, destroyed, never the same. I didn't want that to be the answer, but I was afraid it might be.

Cathi: My dad dying was the only other spiritual crisis as powerful as this. I never felt I'd walk away from God, like Brent's saying, but I felt abandoned by God.

Brent: There was part of me that worried if this didn't work out, I was probably going to walk away from God. Even though, through the tough times, God had always been there for me. Who knew how crazy I might get? This experience could make me crazy enough to walk away from something that important to me.

Cathi: I read my Bible a lot and prayed a lot. But I was terrified of what answers might come from God.

Brent: The class helped us to see scripture—the vital verses— from the perspective of infertility. That was very helpful. Of course, we'd read things like, "God waited until she was 90 to give Sarah children." We didn't want that. But I got an understanding that this could take a while.

Cathi: Our stress level got better with the class, even though it was escalating on the medical side.

Brent: I was still overwhelmed and totally distracted, but the class helped us cope better.

Cathi: The class gave us something to talk about. It gave us a way to structure discussions so we weren't just going around and around saying the same things over and over to each other. It was more productive than us just rambling. It was good to have a foundation—a framework to talk in. Just always talking to each other about the same things was totally counterproductive.

Then, what happened?

Brent: We came up with a plan to start IUI's....

Cathi: … and when they did the ultrasound, they found a cyst. They said, "Hold everything. You have a gigantic cyst." I was totally caught off-guard. I said, "Define gigantic. What does that mean?" They said I couldn't start the drugs until we dealt with this giant, golf-ball-sized cyst.

A month later, the golf ball was bigger and there were lots of mini golf balls. It was definitely problem *not* solved. I ended up having surgery for Stage Three endometriosis.

Brent: We started IVF eight weeks after the surgery—the first week of lacrosse season.

Cathi: It was very stressful. Brent was giving me shots 3-4 times a day. I hadn't told anyone at work. They noticed I kept leaving for the doctor.

I had a blood test on Day 10 after the transfer. Talk about being distracted. I told my boss I needed to work at home that afternoon, so I could get the results call there. The nurse said she'd call around 2 pm.

Brent had the first game of the season that night and un-fortunately, he wouldn't be home until about 10 pm.

Brent: I told her specifically, "Do not call me. I can't handle bad news and coaching a game at the same time."

Cathi: I understood where he was coming from. If it came to it, I envisioned sitting in the bathtub with a bottle of red wine.

Brent: I didn't like leaving Cathi, but I had to. The problem with infertility is no one can know what's going on. If anyone knew, they'd have no problem with me missing a game. But I wasn't going to tell my players or their parents—which meant I had no good excuse not to be there. I'm the head coach. Not being there would be a very big deal.

Cathi: I came home from work to wait for the call. I started convincing myself that it didn't work. I'd had some spotting and I thought, that definitely means it didn't work. Two o'clock rolled around and no call. I had a client call at 3:00. Should I get on the call and distract myself? And do what if my cell phone rang? Make up some fake reason to hang up?

I got on the conference call. Forty-five minutes later, I finished the call and still hadn't heard. I thought, if the nurse doesn't want to call, it's bad news.

So, 4:20 rolls around and the doctor calls me. He said, "I just want to tell you, you're pregnant." I was so floored... I'd been so prepared for the other news.

I said, "Are you sure?"

He said, "Well yeah, I'm pretty sure. I'm looking at the test results right here. That's what you wanted, right?"

I said, "Yeah, but I can't believe it. I've got a bottle of red wine all picked out...."

He said, "Well don't drink it!" At the end of the call, he told me, "You've got to track Brent down."

I said, "He told me not to."

He laughed and said, "That's because he expected bad news."

Brent: He was right. As stressed and frustrated as we were, I was bottling everything up inside. I knew I could end up snapping at a referee or blowing up at one of my kids, and I'd regret it for the rest of my life. So I'd told Cathi, "Don't call me unless you feel like you truly have to."

Cathi: So, I called his cell phone.

Brent: Meanwhile, my assistant coach had asked me on the bus on the way to the game, "When are you guys going to have kids?" I told him, "One of these days." Little did he know we were waiting to hear.

I saw that Cathi had called my cell phone, so I walked way away from everyone else. Of course, I was assuming it was bad news.

When she told me, I was so ecstatic, I ended up telling my assistant coach, "You know that question you asked earlier? I just found out we're pregnant!"

What would you say you learned through this journey?

Brent: The worst part about infertility—especially from the guy's perspective—is that you can't survive it by yourself. You're not strong enough. You're going to fail. You've got to have people around you who truly understand.

It's such a weird thing to talk to people about, but I never regretted telling someone about it. Every time I told somebody, I got some form of compassion. A lot of people I talked to would say, "Yeah, that happened to us, too." Suddenly, they were willing to share their story.

It's so easy to get so isolated. I wish I had told more people sooner. We got to a breaking point where we had to tell people, and that was good. I needed the support. It's not natural for guys to share stuff like this, but you have to do it.

Cathi: I'd been thinking, "A baby is a baby; give it to me now." I learned that God has His timing, and He makes it work. Your baby will be born at a specific time for a specific reason. It's that idea… like Bill Gates being born at the perfect time to fulfill his potential. It's that kind of thing.

I started hearing amazing stories from alumni couples and realized I'd never thought about it that way. I hadn't thought about it from that perspective.

I had no patience. I'd been thinking, "Any baby—just give me a baby and I'll take it from there." Now, I see more of the timing of how everything is supposed to work. It's not just about me. There's a bigger purpose. A bigger plan.

Brent: Before this, I thought I wanted to start a family, and become a school administrator, and… I had a life plan. But now, I don't feel the rush on the career side. It doesn't bother me. If it happens, it happens. I'm not going to force it.

If I'd had my way, it would've been more time at work when we finally had our baby. It wouldn't have been good to take that extra time away from home. Maybe that was part of God's plan.

It's frustrating at times, but I'm getting much better at trusting that there is a long-term plan. It was so good to hear from alumni in the class: "In hindsight, the timing was perfect." If God told me the long-term plan, I'd take it for granted. I'd never learn the lessons I needed to learn—about not being in control, turning things over to God, praying about what matters most….

Cathi: We're going to be different parents now than if we'd succeeded when we first tried. Our relationship is different; it's stronger. And our faith went through a lot; we had to turn things over to God and truly let go. I think there will be a lot of parenting things like that… where we have to turn it over. I'm not sure we'd have the perspective and the comfort level that we do without this experience.

There's really no way to be stronger in your faith if you're never tested.

Finding the Way

Our study of the word "infertile" and the metaphor of fallow fields shows us that God is hard at work—in us, around us, and through us—during the season of active waiting.

It also makes it abundantly clear that God does not intend to enrich our spiritual lives by offering us an easy escape from infertility. Just the opposite. He seems determined to strengthen our faith by placing us squarely in the middle of adversity and then offering us a way through it, with His help.

After the previous lesson, couples can sometimes see pieces of the picture coming together into a unified vision of God's plan and purpose. They realize that, together with God, they are preparing hearts, minds and souls for an abundant future made possible only by the current season of preparation. Can they rest in that knowledge *all* the time? No, but they sense themselves trusting God with growing confidence. And with that trust comes peace.

Why does the fallow field metaphor resonate so powerfully? For women, it is often because so much of the infertility experience has been physical—occurring in bodies that seem to be constantly undergoing "harrowing," plowing," and "harvesting." We can relate to vigilant monitoring of the field (since we are constantly monitoring our own physical sensations), and the idea of life cycles and seasons (since we experience them firsthand within our own bodies).

Both women and men are reassured by the confidence exhibited by God the farmer/gardener. He cares deeply about the harvest. Every choice He makes anticipates the desired end, revealing both wisdom and experience. Recognizing and trusting this is a critical step toward relinquishing control to the One who is truly in control.

But some people struggle with the fallow field metaphor. Although they understand it intellectually, their visceral response is resistance. Most often, it's because they are resisting the passive role of waiting (and waiting, and waiting...) while God works in their lives.

> ● ● ●
>
> Infertility alters our trajectory, forcing us into unfamiliar territory
>
> ● ● ●

Those lives had appeared to be on a perfect trajectory toward a desirable future until infertility altered it. Now, they know only that they're lost and moving deep into unfamiliar territory. They don't want to wait for God to find and rescue them; they want to do something to rescue themselves.

Does that sound familiar? Understandable? Even justified?

Remember Sarah...? She tried to rescue her dream when she sensed her trajectory arcing away from motherhood. She took decisive action, only to learn that impatience and impulsivity led away from God's best.

Can taking action ever be a good choice if we're separated from our dream and feeling lost to God? It depends... on whether we are eager to work **with** God, or just tired of waiting **for** God. It's the difference between initiative in response to God's will, and impatience in response to our own. One path can lead us out of this wilderness; the other will take us deeper into it. How can we tell which is which?

This is where we begin the lesson.

We start with good news: the Bible contains numerous precedents of wilderness wandering as a season of testing and preparation. Moses, David, John the Baptist and Jesus all spent time in physical wildernesses. These symbolized the spiritual challenges they were facing—and would ultimately overcome.

During these wilderness periods, their faith in God's truth was tested under extreme circumstances. They faced physical, emotional and psychological stressors—all within the context of a spiritual showdown between faith and false truth. Each of them found that their radical reliance on God's complete provision strengthened, equipped and sustained them. And, it glorified God.

In the same way, infertility tests our ability to rely on God's truth under extreme circumstances. It separates us from the predictability and control that created an illusion of mastery in our "normal" lives, and plunges us into an uncharted wilderness.

●　　●　　●

Pause and consider.... How has infertility exposed the illusion of control in your former life? Has this brought you to a showdown between faith and false truth? Has it taught you anything about the wisdom of relying on God?

●　　●　　●

Battling infertility forces us to acknowledge our limitations. Then, fully aware of all we cannot do alone, we must somehow overcome those limitations if we are to become parents. The best strategy: radical reliance on God's complete provision. That, of course, is the purpose of this journey. The wilderness experience is an invitation to go deeper with God—to test and prove to ourselves His total reliability and sovereignty.

By showing us how small and helpless we actually are, God enables us to see the size of our need for Him. It is a humbling experience, and one that couples often resent. But in actuality, this is a period of gifting in anticipation of what is coming next. We are being readied. The testing and trials of this wilderness adventure will strengthen our faith, preparing us for the challenges God knows lay ahead.

God wants us to learn humility and God-reliance. He wants us to see clearly that control is a false god. He wants us to recognize that we can't sleepwalk through our lives if we are going to grow in faith—and *that* is His desire for us: a closer walk with Him.

So, although the process is difficult and the journey arduous, we can learn to lean into it… if we understand why it's happening. The purpose of this journey is not just to become parents; it is to strengthen our faith and to glorify God.

What is the wilderness journey like? Authors John Eldredge (*Wild at Heart*) and Bruce Wilkinson (*The Dream Giver*) have written tremendously insightful books on the topic that seem especially compelling to men. Both agree that the wilderness experience is one we would do anything to avoid—but God calls us to it anyway, in order to accomplish His purpose. Both also agree that, in hindsight, the journey is faith-building and life-changing.

> ❋ ❋ ❋
>
> ### The wilderness journey is faith-building & life-changing
>
> ❋ ❋ ❋

Details of the journey vary by person, but common themes emerge when men discuss their wilderness experiences. Some describe it as being like a spiritual Outward Bound. They have no knowledge of what obstacles they'll face—or when. They are painfully aware of their limitations and weaknesses. And yet, they find themselves able to surmount each challenge as it arises. God consistently meets their needs, as they appear, while also revealing a deep reservoir of strength in and through Him.

As they make their way through the wilderness, these men rely increasingly on a growing confidence that God knows this territory. Ultimately, they come to find confidence in the Bible's instruction: "Trust God from the bottom of your heart;

don't try to figure out everything on your own. Listen for God's voice in everything you do, everywhere you go; *he's the one who will keep you on track"* [Proverbs 3:5-6, Message, italics added].

Others describe the wilderness experience as a time of concentrated focus. The crutches and enablers that usually reinforce self-reliance are stripped away. Unable to lean on these supports, humbled by uncertainty and powerlessness, these men seek a new source of strength.

They pray with a passion borne of desperation. Eager to hear from the One who can teach them what is happening and why, they listen with a deepened desire for understanding. They find themselves exploring their relationship with God in a new way, and with an intensity previously unimaginable. And, they find themselves more willing to be obedient as their trust in God's faithfulness grows.

● ● ●

Pause and consider.... How has your wilderness experience thus far altered your relationship with God? Is it more challenging? More rewarding? Do you see ways in which God is using this journey to draw nearer to you?

● ● ●

These wilderness stories offer both encouragement and insight to those of us in the midst of the journey. We are not trapped in the wilderness indefinitely; *there is a way out*. Others have made this journey, and we can learn from their experience.

So, how did they navigate their way through unfamiliar terrain? How did they get their bearings and set a course? And what advice can they offer those still struggling to find a way through and onward?

When asked, those who have completed the infertility journey consistently recommend a specific light, map, and compass.

From a spiritual standpoint, each of us journeys through the wilderness alone. But, we still experience it in ways that are similar to those who have gone before us. For this reason, the Bible's wilderness stories cast a *light* in the darkness. They equip us with knowledge of our ancestors' histories and God's role in them. By studying these, we learn that God can be trusted, that He always provides for His people, and that the path of the righteous shines ever brighter [Proverbs 4:18].

Similarly, alumni of our infertility Bible study (who frequently return to share accounts of their own wilderness experiences) speak directly into the hearts of those currently wandering and lost. Their stories are illuminating; they pass a torch of hope and inspiration from those who recently traversed this spiritual territory to those still struggling to make their way.

The Bible promises, "Light is shed upon the righteous and joy on the upright in heart" [Psalm 97:11]. Often, it is through the testimonies of these alumni that this promise begins to be fulfilled for the couples in our study.

The Bible is our map for this spiritual journey

The entire Bible serves as a *map* for this spiritual journey. As with any map, it does us no good unless we open it, examine it, and identify the relevant landmarks that indicate we are moving closer to the destination.

As we study it, we find that the Bible's stories map out every thought or emotion that will arise during this quest: anger, grief, loneliness, heartache, anguish, impatience, hope, confusion, hostility, panic, sadness, resignation, shame, desperation, lethargy, despair, guilt, urgency, failure, fear, resentment, uncertainty, disappointment, defiance, hopelessness....None of these are unfamiliar to God. He knows this territory.

It is important to remember that the Bible's stories also map routes for coming to God with intense emotions. We cannot have an intimate relationship with One whom we do not trust.

We cannot receive the grace, love or peace we need to make our way through this if we have hardened our hearts with anger, or in fear.

Armed with this knowledge, we can delve into an honest exploration of this wilderness. We can expose thoughts and feelings we have previously denied or suppressed—and in so doing, invite God to comfort, strengthen and guide us.

●　　●　　●

Pause and consider.... Have you ever thought of the Bible as a map from God? Have you tried using it as one? Might that constitute taking action to save yourself and find your way? If so, does that affect your desire to spend time studying it?

●　　●　　●

The Bible tells us, "above all else, guard your heart for it is the wellspring of life" [Proverbs 4:23]. This is an active instruction. We are called to *do* something, even as God is working in and through us, guiding our steps along this journey.

How?

We are to trust that God wants the best for His people. That He is not the enemy. That He is the God of hope, of purpose, of renewal, of joy, of blessing, and of life. That He is at work in our wilderness experience—right now. And, that He has provided a map to help us find our way.

When we choose to trust God's leadership in this journey, we stop struggling to regain control. We stop deal-making and second-guessing. Instead, we rest in the knowledge that the shepherd of the Bible's 23rd Psalm will lead us "in paths of righteousness." Those paths will bring us to the "hope and a future" He has planned specifically to bless us.

Our role is to step out in faith.

How does God guide our steps "in the way that we should go"? The Holy Spirit becomes our internal *compass*—the voice that tells us to turn this way, the impulse that nudges us to find another path, the sudden sense that we should revisit the map, or the realization that this is a good place to rest and recuperate before pressing on again.

Even though we do not know the way through this wilderness, we discover we can rely on this internal compass to guide our steps. God will lead us by the power of the Holy Spirit, and we can work with Him by following that lead. This is the way through the wilderness.

Which way will *you* choose through this wilderness: defiance or reliance?

Throughout this journey, as we become increasingly aware that God can provide all that we need, we are brought—again and again—to a choice: Which way will we choose through the wilderness? Will we choose willful defiance of God's guidance? Or, will we choose to trust in humble reliance on Him?

We can resist the truth God is trying to reveal to us and remain lost indefinitely, or we can embrace it and be led by God through this wilderness to our desired destination.

Will choosing humility require feeble dependence? Thankfully, no. God wants us to be strong *in Him*—full of purpose and passion, confidence and wisdom. So, God meets us in the wilderness, equips us with all that we need, and instructs us (through the apostle Paul) to "put on the armor of God"—the belt of truth, the breastplate of righteousness, the shield of faith, the helmet of salvation, and the sword that is the word of God [Ephesians 6:14-17]. These will enable us to fight every spiritual battle en route to our goal, and ultimately, to reach it according to His will.

"What lessons from the wilderness experience can we carry forward as parents?" This question incorporates so many assumptions, it sometimes seems to paralyze couples' thinking. They wonder: *Am I in a wilderness experience? Am I learning any lessons? Will I ever be a parent? If so, will I remember what*

I've learned? Will it even matter at that point?

"Yes" is the answer to all these questions.

God's plan to give us *what* we need now (experiences) in order to be *who* we need to be later (as parents) means that the lessons we're learning will be useful. And applicable. Reviewing what we've learned thus far, along with lessons previous infertile "travelers" have learned, enables us to project forward in time—to a day when we, too, will reach the end of this journey and apply what we have learned to our new role as parents.

●   ●   ●

Pause and consider.... Which lessons from your experience might be helpful to you as a parent? Is it possible that God planned these? That they're not accidental? If so, would that change the way you see your infertility journey? How so?

●   ●   ●

What are the lessons that will benefit us most in our future role as parents?

For one, the wilderness journey teaches us that a spiritual struggle is a gift. This well-disguised blessing makes us stronger—in faith, and in wisdom. We would never ask or hope for such a difficult challenge because this process is so painful. But through it, God reveals His faithfulness to us. That is a lesson we must carry forward.

The infertility journey also teaches us that we may set out feeling empty-handed and ill-prepared, but God consistently equips us in real time. He knows what we need, when we need it, and how to deliver it to us in a way that reveals His hand—thus renewing our confidence in His faithfulness.

Remembering this will help us see Him, seek His help, and trust His goodness more readily in the future. It will remind us to live confidently by faith, even when we feel lost.

During this journey, we learn the importance of thankful

hearts that take nothing for granted. We have known deep long-ing, but we have also received timely provisions—again and again.

* * *

God provides manna in many forms to nourish, empower and sustain us

* * *

God has provided manna to us in many forms—both tangible and intangible—to nour-ish, empower and sustain us. More than just in-suring our survival in this wilderness, that manna has served to remind us of His presence, His goodness, and His protection. We are His people, and we are never lost to Him.

This wilderness wandering teaches us to choose mindfully. We have faced the choice between self-reliance and God-reliance, and seen the consequences. We have learned that seeing with eyes of faith enables us to see a path that is otherwise impossible to identify.

We have experienced an internal leading that urges, "go this way," "try this," or "turn here." We know with deepening certainty that we would not make our way through this unfami-liar territory without our faithful guide, the Holy Spirit.

Along the way, we have also learned the importance of sensitivity and compassion for other travelers. We have felt the sting of isolation and heartache of loneliness. We have expe-rienced the fear of unending darkness and insurmountable obstacles. But, we have also received the gift of hope and encouragement. Having found strength by faith, we recognize the need to extend ourselves and share that strength with others who are struggling.

This journey teaches us that God has His own perfect timing. In this wilderness, we see aspects of life in the Kingdom of God with fresh eyes. We see the interrelatedness of all things God creates. We understand how small we are, and how great God is. And, sooner or later, we do come to experience God's perfect timing with great joy.

We learn a lot from this one journey.

Most of all, again and again, we learn that God is faithful. As the Psalmist writes, "…The Lord is good and His love endures forever; his faithfulness continues through all generations" [Psalm 100:5]. This is the great lesson of the wilderness journey. It is the one we must pass on to the next generation, in our role as stewards of the souls entrusted to us.

Having lived it ourselves, having experienced it with such emotional intensity, we will be able to pass this truth on with conviction and certainty. We will know it to be so with every fiber of our being, and our children will receive this knowledge as a gift from God.

So, is the way through the wilderness a straight line once we learn these lessons from our predecessors? No, not usually. Once we apply them to our lives? Not necessarily. Is there a finite amount of time any of us will have to wander before God leads us through, and the journey ends? No. Then how do we find genuine hope out in the middle of a spiritual No Man's Land?

Jesus said, "I will not leave you as orphans; I will come to you. On that day you will realize that I am in my Father, and you are in me, and I am in you. He who loves me will be loved by my Father, and I, too, will love him and show myself to him" [John 14:18, 20-21].

• • •

How do we find genuine hope in the middle of a spiritual No Man's Land?

• • •

We are not given knowledge of the future; God alone knows those details. We don't know how near or far we are from the edge of our spiritual wilderness—how close we are to home… to "hope and a future"… to conceiving or adopting the child we long to welcome.

But, we are given knowledge of God's love and His faithfulness. We are given Jesus' own words to enable us to hear God's voice and understand His will. And, we are given "the Spirit of truth… (who) lives with you and will be in you" [John

14:17].

We are **never** alone or abandoned in the wilderness. We are constantly under the loving protection and guidance of the Trinity—Father, Son and Holy Spirit. Jesus counsels us, "Do not let your hearts be troubled. Trust in God; trust also in me" [John 14:1]. That is the greatest challenge, and the great invitation, of this wilderness journey.

The outcome is assured; God already knows the precise day and moment when we will meet our child for the first time. He knows who that child will be, and why he or she will have been entrusted specifically to us.

Can we trust Him? Will we move forward on this journey with confident hope—focused not on the size of our obstacles, but on the size of our God?

The Bible says, "As you know, we consider blessed those who have persevered. You have heard of Job's perseverance and have seen what the Lord finally brought about. The Lord is full of compassion and mercy" [James 5:11]. Equipped with this knowledge, we can press on toward that future moment, confident that our perseverance will be blessed.

●　　●　　●

Pause and consider.... How would you describe your level of confidence that your perseverance will be blessed? Did the wilderness metaphor in this lesson affect that confidence? In what ways? How can you apply what you've discovered?

●　　●　　●

Reflections

Kirsten & Mike

How did your story begin?

Kirsten: We met in a church singles' Sunday school class. Mike was the president and I was the treasurer. We were both in our mid-30's. We got engaged after six months, and married nine months after that. We got pregnant after just three months of trying.

My Navy Reserve unit deployed to Iraq and I was left in charge of the folks that were still here in the United States. Shortly before my unit returned, I started having a lot of bleeding. The doctor said, "Why don't you meet me at the hospital."

Mike: I remember going to the hospital and it being very much a blur. I remember the nurse tried to find a heartbeat in the womb, and she couldn't find one. We both thought, "She just doesn't know what she's doing." We were in such denial.

We thought, "The doctor will get here and it'll be okay." He got there and it wasn't okay. He left the room and a minute later, the baby came.

Kirsten: It was a spontaneous miscarriage at almost 20 weeks. A little boy.

Mike: I had to run out of the room to get the doctor. He ran in and four nurses ran in after him. I remember standing out in the hallway feeling very dizzy. One of the nurses got a chair for me and said, "It's okay. Just sit here." I didn't think I was going to recover. But somehow, a feeling of calm came over me and I heard a voice in my head saying, "Go to Kirsten."

Kirsten: I don't think I even knew you were ever someplace else. All I remember is you being right there with me.

Mike: Somehow, I went from not being able to stand up, to being able to be with her. I was only sitting for about five seconds. It makes me think of that passage about the footprints in the sand....

When a nurse grabs you and puts you in a chair, it's because she doesn't think you can stand. I was spiraling completely out of control. But somehow, I stood up and went back in there. One moment, I was dizzy... but then one second later, I was clear-headed and able to function. I don't think the human mind has the ability to reboot like that. I tell you, that'll make you believe in divine grace.

Kirsten: It turned out I miscarried because of a clotting disorder. The placenta ruptured. We came home the next day, and I remember Mike and I were just huddled up together on the couch. We didn't know what else to do.

When you go through a miscarriage midway through a pregnancy, a huge hole opens up in your life. You feel completely isolated. You know in your mind that other people have gone through this, but you never expect it to happen to you.

The doctor said, "Next month, you can start trying again," but emotionally, we were definitely not ready.

Mike: The next two years were the worst two years of my life. It took every bit of emotional strength to get through it.

Kirsten: We tried getting pregnant again the old-fashioned way. When that didn't work, we did four IUI's. The results were always negative. The number of follicles was always dismal. The doctors said, "We need to go to IVF."

Mike: During those two years, she was nuts. She was hitting herself and saying, "I'm worthless." It was really tough. In my spiritual life, it was the antithesis of that moment when God had carried me. This was like I was in the desert. That's what it felt like.

Kirsten: The first IVF cycle didn't work. We didn't get any embryos and there was no transfer. We had our follow-up appointment and they didn't say, "We can't help you." They said, "You can't be helped."

Mike: The doctor literally said to us, "You will never have kids." After she dropped that on us, she looked at me and asked, "Do you think your wife is depressed?"

I said, "No, I think she's grieving." But I was thinking, what kind of bizarre world are we in?!

Kirsten: We figured out later that they had their protocol—and they got great results with certain people with that model. But we didn't fit that model. Rather than saying, "Another model might fit you," they essentially said, "Our model is clearly the best and if it doesn't work, nothing will."

Mike: Then, I had another God-works-in-mysterious-ways experience. A doctor we consulted said, "If you're serious about IVF, you should see the top guy at Cornell." So, we went there and did a completely different IVF protocol—and it was a dismal failure. Terrible results. One follicle. It wasn't even worth doing a retrieval.

We were checking out of the hotel after having been there for three weeks. The guy at the desk saw that I wasn't looking happy. He said, "You guys were here for IVF, weren't you?"

I said, "Yeah, it didn't go very well."

Then he said, "Let me tell you: it's going to work out for

you guys." I looked at him and thought, you don't know what you're talking about. He said, "Sometimes, you just look at people and you know. I know it's going to work for you."

Kirsten: And that stayed with you.

Mike: About two weeks later, I was getting ready to go to work and I had another "eureka" moment. As I stood there, all of a sudden I realized that I could love a girl from China as my daughter. And I felt calm. That was the first time in two years that I had felt calm.

I thought: it's a choice. I'm going to choose to have a family and if that means adopting a girl from China, then I'll love her as my daughter. I'll make that choice and I won't have a regret about it.

Kirsten wasn't there yet. She wasn't ready for that. So, we got into the donor egg program. We actually picked somebody out from a California agency.

Kirsten: Off the internet.

Mike: They wanted me to write a letter to this person. Well, of all the I-would-never-have-imagined moments, that was right up there.

Then, we talked to the Cornell doctor. He wanted to try a hybrid protocol for one more IVF.

Kirsten: I remember saying, "I want one more shot at this." I needed a period on the end of the sentence that said: this will not work. I needed to be sure.

Mike: She doubted that an adopted child would feel like her daughter. That's how much her biological/hormonal stuff was affecting her thinking

Kirsten: There's a very different process going on for a woman than a man. I felt something deep down inside of me—like a push—that completely overwhelmed me and took total control of my life and my mind. I had incredible energy in the quest for a baby. It was so intense that it was impossible to control. I think God was in that.

Mike: So, we were on our way to a church Thanksgiving event when we got a call from New York saying we need you here to-morrow. I'd had enough at that point. I said, "What are you talking about? What do you mean you need us there?"

The nurse said, "You got this result and that result... and it's all good, and it's a go. So, come on."

I said, "Look, you need to tell me. Is there a real chance? I know there are no sure things, and not even any probables, but is this more than one-in-a-million?"

She said, "These numbers look pretty good. You should come on out." So, we went to the party and felt like we had the biggest secret in the world.

We hopped on a plane the next morning. I immediately got the flu and was in bed all week. I had to play my part at the end of the week—in a cup—and then I went back to bed. Two days later, the retrieval was amazing news.

Kirsten: I woke up from the retrieval and they said, "We got ten eggs." I said, "Are you sure? From me? Are you sure those are my results?"

And then a couple days later, we heard we had five embryos. Again, I said, "Are you sure? Embryos?!" Because we hadn't gotten to that point with any of the previous experiences.

Mike: Here's another God story. While we were waiting for the results of the transfer, my law firm had a holiday dinner. Kirsten had been spotting, and she was worried. My paralegal, who has a PhD in theology, leaned over to me and said, "I think it's going to work out. Everything's fine."

Certain people and what they say to you... their voice stands out for a reason. Hers was one of those. At the time, you look at them like a crazy person—like I did with the guy in New York—but it sticks with you. It was said in a way that led me to believe that this person knew.

Other people try to say nice things, but they don't know what's going to happen to you. But these people, they know. And you can tell. They're like a prophet. They're telling you things are going to be okay.

Kirsten: The next day, I was waiting to hear the results. My phone rang, and I thought, take a deep breath because I was thinking it was going to be more bad news.

They said, "You're pregnant."

I remember saying, "What? Are you sure?" I called Mike and I can't remember if we celebrated. We were kind of in shock. But a positive, calm feeling came over me.

Mike: Now, there was hope.

Kirsten: Then, they told us there were three sacs…

Mike: … and I almost fell down. The nurses were joking about two boys and a girl, or two girls and a boy…. But, someone had told us at the beginning of this process, "Three is not a good number for you." They didn't just say that, they said basically, "You'd need to abort one." So, my mind went right to: This isn't good news any more. How could we make that decision after everything we'd been through?

Fortunately, it turned out one of the sacs was empty.

I didn't exhale until the babies came—a boy and a girl. Actually, until they were about three months old.

What role did the infertility Bible study play in your story?

Mike: It was great to meet other people in the same situation. But, at the end of the first class, there were several people crying. I didn't know if that was good—reopening wounds.

Then, we went the second time and there was a huge

difference. People had been so sad and it had been so heavy. But this time, it was entirely different and the tone was so positive. It was much more hopeful.

Then, over time, one couple adopted. We got pregnant with IVF. Other people did it the old-fashioned way. Things started happening to the group as a whole. It changed. There was hope.

Sometimes, alumni would come back to encourage couples. We did that. There was one woman who was talking to the group about trying to adopt and how it was so hard. She wasn't sure when she met the birth mother if it was going to be a good fit. She started crying as she was telling this story.

I looked at her and said, "You're not gonna believe me, but I know this is all gonna work out for you. I don't know if it's going to be this child, but it will work out." Like the guy in New York did for me.

I don't know why I said that and felt so confident—other than I was inspired by God. I felt at that moment that it *was* going to work out and I should tell her. She adopted a child within a few months. It was interesting to be on the other side of the fence and say something… to give hope.

What lessons did you learn from your experience?

Kirsten: If I had known that becoming a parent wasn't just my plan, it was God's plan, I would've been able to let go and not be so stressed during that two-year period. That's definitely part of the challenge: trusting – but not knowing God's plan.

Mike: I agree! After our twins were born, we thought that was it; we were done. But God wasn't done. Kirsten got pregnant again – naturally – and now the twins have a sib.

If I've learned anything, it's to trust God's plan.

Living a Legacy

When we begin our last lesson, couples often experience a surge of mixed emotions. They have felt understood in our group—some, for the first time on this difficult journey. They have shared their fears and vulnerabilities, and had a chance to care for wounded hearts. They have received Jesus' invitation, "Come to me, all you who are weary and burdened, and I will give you rest" [Matthew 11:28]. They have responded and experienced periods of peace—moments, hours, even days—that had previously seemed so elusive.

They have also found companionship on a journey that, from the world's vantage point, has looked daunting, depressing and even hopeless. Now, each participant's perspective has begun to shift to a more grace-filled one. They have come to realize that their suffering is temporary—even though it feels unending—and that it has a purpose. This knowledge has led them to embrace the promise that God, the dream-giver, has plans for "hope and a future."

At the same time, in these weeks together, most couples have also been through at least one heartbreaking cycle. Some have miscarried. Some have learned that IVF has failed. Some have not been chosen to adopt the child they were convinced was destined for them. And yet, they have all continued to cling to a hope that does not die, despite evidence that continues to suggest their dream may never be reality.

No wonder there are so many intense, mixed emotions at this last meeting.

Are these couples ready to set out again? To continue the journey? We begin our last lesson where we first started, face-to-face with the fact of infertility.

●   ●   ●

Pause and consider.... How has the time with these lessons been for you...? Affirming and uplifting? Or, disturbing and emotional? Maybe a combination of the two? How do you feel approaching this last lesson? Relieved, apprehensive, a mix of both...? How are your thoughts or feelings different from when you began this journey?

●   ●   ●

By this last lesson, most couples still struggle to explain their experience to anyone who hasn't been lost in this particular wilderness. There's the feeling of being a wounded survivor, despite the lack of visible scars; the seemingly irrational need to keep trying to reach the desired destination, despite what it has already cost in time, money and heartache; and, the fact that infertility can and does feel like a curse, no matter what the Bible says.

No amount of insightful, inspired Bible study can protect couples fully from the painful parts of the infertility experience. No amount of living mindfully in the Kingdom of God can insulate anyone completely from feelings of despair, grief or unbearable loss.

Has this study served any meaningful purpose then? Yes, I tell them. Just as it has for you.

It has delivered the promises God has made to generations of believers, directly to His beloved children. It has spoken the truth of those promises into your soul and called you to a deeper, richer faith life. It has enabled you to see, with eyes of faith, the good that God is doing in your life, right now. And, it has equipped you to put on the armor of God—the belt of truth, the breastplate of righteousness, the shield of faith, the helmet of salvation, and the sword of the Spirit—to fight off doubt and despair.

Just as Jesus spoke words of hope to his disciples, he has spoken them to you. God has also. And, the Holy Spirit has been sent to dwell within your mind and heart, constantly reminding you of this hope—encouraging you, sustaining you, strengthening you [I Corinthians 3:16, II Corinthians 13:14].

Despite what the world sees and understands, you know you carry inside you a God-given seed of hope. So, now what? If there is still no baby, what does that mean? What should you do, knowing that more cycles of hope-anticipation-despair may lie ahead?

You should claim God's promises and live into them... as if you already know with certainty that God's will is done. Jesus taught this to his disciples, saying, "...whatever you ask for in prayer, believe that you have received it, and it will be yours" [Mark 11:24]. He did not say, it will happen instantly. And he did not mean to imply that God grants every wish. He was teaching that, *when our desire aligns with God's will*, it shall be done.

So, lift up your head and look past this moment. These many months—even years—of struggling to conceive or adopt will end exactly the way God intends. He has put you on this path for a reason. Trust in His wisdom, claim that promise, and press on.

● ● ●

When our desire aligns with God's will, it shall be done

● ● ●

Will you conceive a baby one day? Will it be the way you've imagined—a perfect pregnancy followed by happily ever after? Maybe not. Are you willing to trust that, if it's a different story, God's plan will be better? Realize that "better" may not mean easier or consistently happier, but better for your spiritual growth, your child's unique needs, or both. Better for God's purpose, and for His Kingdom.

Consider this… several couples who have participated in our study have given birth to children with health issues or special needs. Several sets of twins have been born, and more twins have been adopted. In each of these cases, God entrusted children who needed "above and beyond" effort (time, energy and finances) to parents who were committed to doing whatever it took to meet their children's needs.

Might this period of waiting be strengthening your desire and commitment for a similar reason? If that is what God has planned for you, are you ready to say, "yes"? Will you trust Him, no matter what—or when—the plan? If so, you delight Him because you put your faith in His plan above your need to control the outcome. In so doing, you align yourself more completely with His will.

● ● ●

Be open to God's leading. Where is His path taking you?

● ● ●

So now, be open to God's leading. A child may not come into your life the way you've imagined. Can you trust God enough to allow for that possibility? Do you need to let go of your vision of time as a pregnant couple—or hold that vision more loosely? Are you willing to consider adoption? Foster parenting? Life with a foreign-born child? A special needs child? Multiples?

What about some other means of establishing a deeply meaningful place in the life of a child? Is there an interim step God wants you to take before you become a parent?

What does the Holy Spirit, your internal compass, point you toward? Where do you feel God's path taking you?

He has a plan that will lead your life to intersect with the life of a child who needs you. That is why He placed the seed of hope in your heart. That is why He has nurtured and protected it, even as you have suffered through loss after grief after heartache. He will execute His plan perfectly (if you do not willfully alter its course), as soon as all the pieces are in place.

If you can trust God's purposefulness, then even in the absence of detailed knowledge, you can rest assured that everything you have experienced, lost and gained during this season of infertility has been for a reason. God has been, and of course, continues to be, at work preparing the future He intends for you and a particular child or children.

● ● ●

Pause and consider.... Do you sense your mind and heart opening to a broader array of possibilities? Does that make it any easier to let go of the need to control your story? What insights has God given you recently?

● ● ●

While you await the future God has planned, you have work to do—and an opportunity to start doing it. God wants you to be developing the heart and mind of a faithful steward. He is equipping you now, through this experience. He is providing you opportunities to strengthen your faith, your resilience, your trust and your courage. He is teaching you that hope does not depend on what the world sees, but on what can be seen with eyes of faith.

So, live what you are learning. Think of it as legacy living—making choices *today* that build a firmer, better foundation for a child's future. God wants your passion for parenting sometime in the future to translate into words and actions that reflect His priorities *today*. Is that happening?

Examine your life and your choices. Do they reflect your trust in God's provision? His timing? His purposefulness? Do you feel a sense of accountability for the blessings that have already been entrusted to you? Are you a good steward of those blessings? Do you "pay it forward" so others can also experience God's goodness? What about your priorities? Where do you invest your time and treasure?

Make choices that reflect your confidence in God's promise to bring you "hope and a future." Rather than living with a scarcity mentality and a focus on self, live into God's faithfulness with a spirit of abundance. Jesus taught, "...do not worry about your life..." because God will provide all that you need, *with pleasure* [Luke 12:22, italics added]. Trusting that promise, live with a spirit of thankfulness that anticipates joy.

• • •

Live like a steward who is worthy of ever-greater responsibility

• • •

Lay a foundation of healthy relationships, a healthy lifestyle, and most of all, a healthy spiritual life. God intends for you to make good use of every gift He gives you: time, money, freedom, opportunity.... He has given you many gifts prior to a child for a reason. Express your gratitude and live like a steward worthy of ever-greater responsibility. Doing so is an investment in your family's future, and it will be part of your legacy to your child.

Remember, you are part of a chain of blessing that extends from the Old Testament into the New Testament, and then leaps off the page into our world. Part of your role as a steward will be to keep this chain of blessing intact for the next generation. Are you prepared to connect your child to the promises made to all of us through scripture so long ago?

• • •

Pause and consider.... How has the "chain of blessing" brought you to this moment? Are you living the life of a good steward, ready to connect the next generation to scripture's promises? Is God leading you to make any changes in your life?

• • •

"...We know that in all things God works for the good of those who love him, who have been called according to his purpose" [Romans 8:28]. This is the legacy of all believers, across time and throughout generations. It is the promise you will pass on to your descendants, and it will be grounded in the truth of your infertility experience.

Live into this promise.

Soon enough, a child will step into your life story as evidence that God has heard your prayers, delighted in your trust, blessed you, made you a family as He deemed best, and woven you together into the fabric of the narrative that reaches deep into the Old Testament past—and will extend far into the future. That day *is* coming.

Reflections

Laura & Brian

How did your story begin?

Laura: I married Brian when I was 23 and he was 34. I grew up in church. But when we got married, we weren't really active in church.

Brian: We went, but we weren't connecting with people. All the newlyweds in the Sunday School classes were having babies, and so we never really fit in those groups. And there was our age differential. We just weren't finding our place.

Laura: We'd been married for a couple years when we started trying to have kids. And it wasn't happening... and it wasn't happening. I was a schoolteacher and everybody was asking me, "When are you going to get pregnant?" Saying things like, "Why don't you have any kids yet?"

So, I went to the OB and was put on higher and higher doses of Clomid. Fortunately, I have a very good husband who still loved me through all the effects of...

Brian:..... the Crazy Pill!

Laura: All during this time, infertility was becoming a very sensitive subject for other people to talk to me about. My friends and I didn't talk about it a lot. I would cry at home.

Brian: She started getting very concerned about it. I wasn't in a particular hurry to have children and since she was relatively young, I didn't think we had to worry. I was in my mid-30's, so I was ready—but I wasn't worried that this was a problem.

Still, when we weren't getting pregnant and things were not happening—as they started upping the doses of Clomid—it started getting burdensome. She was getting very frustrated.

Laura: 150 milligrams of Clomid?! I mean, my whole side of the bed was wet. I was sweating, having blurred vision… it was so much and I was like, this isn't right.

Brian: Combine that with all the ovulation kits and thermometers….

Laura: I had already spent a lot of money on a computerized $300 dollar thing that tells you when you're ovulating…

Brian: … so, the alarm was going off at 6 am telling her to take her temperature and write it down every day. We were doing *all* this stuff that was disrupting our lives and none of it was working.

Then, the church bulletin came in the mail with a story about a couple starting an infertility Bible study. I was worried this was going to feed into her concern that we had a big problem and increase our stress level. But, I also thought, "Here are some other people who are dealing with this, and we don't have a group at church, and this is something that relates to our situation." So, I showed it to her.

Laura: I said, "We should go to this."

Brian: The church bulletin reached us right at the time when we needed some kind of signal to go. By the time the class started, she was on such a high level of Clomid—they kept increasing and increasing it, and she kept having more and more side effects —that she was very emotional. When she's upset, I'm upset.

Both of us needed an outlet for our stress.

Laura: So we went, not knowing what to expect.

Brian: What we got out of that initial Bible study was a sense of connectedness, like, "Hey, some other people are dealing with this. We *can* talk about this." We also received some very good feedback about our process and about good doctors to go to. Then, after the class,...

Laura: ...I met a girl who told me about her infertility experts. Brian actually called that group of doctors and normally they book 4-8 weeks in advance. Well, they had an opening for us the next day.

Brian: These doctors knew what to look for. They knew what to test for.

Laura: They checked me properly. We found out that the OB had been overstimulating me with Clomid. I had eight enlarged follicles that were about to turn into cysts.

Brian: We were being mis-treated. The OBs thought they were being helpful, but this could have been bad. If she had released those eggs, we could've ended up with a situation where... litters are fine for dogs, but not for humans.

Laura: We needed an expert, someone who understood that every problem is unique and individualized. Getting with a doctor who knows what to look for and how to treat you is critical. They said, "You're ovulating. You're producing follicles. That's not your problem. You are *over*stimulated."

Brian: Then, they talked about all the hormones that come into play and we got educated about reproductive endocrinology like we never imagined. But the important thing was that they understood there's more to infertility than just one variable. And they told us, "We're going to figure this out." That gave us great peace of mind.

Laura: The eight follicles turned into cysts, so I had to go back on birth control—which seemed like a step in the wrong direction....

Brian: .... backwards....

Laura: ... and seemed to defeat the purpose for a couple of months. Then, I was diagnosed with Polycystic Ovarian Syndrome. I am not a typical candidate for PCOS, but I was diagnosed with it. They put me on Metforman and Letrozole, which is kind of like Clomid but with less risk of multiples.

Brian: One of those drugs is usually for diabetics and one is for breast cancer patients, but the doctors knew how to use them to help her.

Laura: We tried to get pregnant on our own using those; that didn't work. Then, we did two IUI's and they didn't work. The second IUI, we found out on Valentine's Day that we were not pregnant. It was a very sad Valentine's Day.

Brian: Was that the day we were at Lowe's?

Laura: Yes.

Brian: We were picking out paint colors and kind of killing time while we were waiting for the call from our doctor's office. I literally had to stand in the aisle and take her tears on my shoulder as the people at Lowe's passed by.

Laura: It couldn't have been any less private.

Brian: We were imagining what people were saying as they walked by us, wondering why Laura was so upset about choosing paint.

Laura: We went home and our doctor said, "Why don't you come in and we'll discuss things?" When we met with him, he said, "We don't know why you're not getting pregnant. You're one of those 10% couples where the infertility is for unknown reasons."

Brian: I had a varicocele repair... we did *everything*, all the way to the end. But we ended up in that 10% unknown. They still didn't know what our problem was.

Laura: So, we decided to try in vitro.

Brian: Laura responded extremely well to all the medications that stimulated egg production. (Laughing) The doctor called her a cheap date.

Laura: I was hyperstimulated; we had 29 eggs. But we didn't want a lot in the freezer.

Brian: Twenty-nine eggs took us into the whole bioethics dilemma.

Laura: That was very much an issue for us. Fortunately, we both agreed on how we felt.

Brian: We were absolutely on the same page.

Laura: I will say that I was very prayerful about this. I was praying every step of the way. I did not want to have a lot of embryos in the freezer. What if you get twelve embryos? We felt like we needed to give them...

Brian: ... any egg that fertilized and made it to implant stage, we felt we had to take it all the way. So, if we had twelve in the freezer and we got twins on the first go round...

Laura: ...we could be looking at fourteen children!

Brian: Possibly. Mathematically. It was unlikely, but still, you have to be prepared for that.

Laura: And we didn't feel that we could ever give them away because those are our children.

Brian: We couldn't give them away. We couldn't leave them in a freezer forever. If we conceived them, we had to give every one of them their chance. We had to trust that God would be in control of how that all turned out.

Laura: Meanwhile, I was always praying for the perfect number. We didn't know what that number was, but I was praying for whatever God had in mind for us. I was just totally giving it to God, every step of the way: "I trust in you. I trust in you."

Brian: So when they retrieved 29 eggs, we were about to…. I was about to hyperventilate! Of course, the medical group jumped on it, "Oh, we're going to get a baby for sure with 29 eggs." But, I can do the math. If two-thirds of them fertilize, and half of them of develop… that's still a lot.

I made the embryologist come out of his office—and he was mad at me for interrupting his work—but I actually made him come talk to me. Because we didn't want 10 babies, or 20 babies, or 29 babies.

Laura: We didn't want that many embryos.

Brian: So, the embryologist actually came out and I argued with him about how many eggs we were even going to fertilize. He gave me all the statistics, and I gave him all the ethical issues. We talked for a long time. Ultimately, we decided to fertilize twenty.

Laura: They injected the sperm into the egg on fifteen of them and let the other five swim around, which was also diagnostic because they could tell if the sperm were breaking through. Well, out of fifteen, twelve fertilized. And out of the five that were free-swimming, three fertilized.

Brian: It was the exact fertilization rate that we'd been quoted. But, we were back at the ethical problem.

Laura: All of this happened on Brian's birthday. So, Day Three came and they called and said, "Out of your fifteen, nine have developed." I came in that day for the transfer. They put two back, so that left me with seven.

Well, on Day Five, I had gone back to work and I was teaching. My kids were in Art and, I'll never forget this, the embryologist called and said, "None of your other embryos survived. None of them made it to blastocyst. You have none left."

At this point, I didn't know if the IVF had worked. I didn't know if I'd get pregnant. I had gone from 29 eggs to none. Right after that call, I had to go pick up my kids from Art. I was literally biting the insides of my cheeks to keep from crying.

Then, I heard God say to me, "Laura, you've prayed about this. Let it go. Trust me." So, I said, "OK." Now, that didn't stop the tears from falling when I called Brian, or my mom....

Brian: Laura's much more spiritually passionate than I am; I'm much more cerebral and scientific. So all along, I was on top of all the numbers, the drugs, what was statistically likely, the chemistry and biology of what was happening.

At that point, when we knew we had no surviving embryos, that Sunday, we were in church. I'd never had a blinding light, burning bush, God-speak-to-me experience..., but I remember sitting in church and this thing—almost like a wave—came across me and said, "Everything's OK. It's going to be fine." I've never had that kind of experience before.

I believed what happened was real. So, I kept telling Laura, "It's going to be fine." She'd ask me, "How do you know?" I'd tell her, "God told me." And when I said that, I really meant it.

Laura: A week and a half later, I went to the doctor to do a blood test. I was bawling. Brian looked like the ultimate insensitive husband because he'd seen all the tears and heard all I could possibly say, and there was nothing more he could do. I sat there crying while he flipped pages in a magazine.

Then they said, "You're pregnant."

Brian: Of course, we would take twins, but we really wanted just one. And that's what we got. We didn't want lots of embryos left in the freezer. We didn't want lots of kids all at once. So, out of all that controversy, and all the ethical debates, and the fights with the embryologist, and Laura's worry and tears... we got the perfect number for us. One.

Laura: Just like I'd prayed for—the perfect number for us. And I give all the glory to God.

What was neat about it is that after we had the baby, thirteen months later we were gearing up to do this again. I called the doctor and set the appointment. It was a little early, but we wanted to get started, not knowing how long it might take.

Brian: We wanted to map out a strategy for baby #2. We assumed we'd have to go all the way to in vitro again, so what were the steps along the way? That's what we wanted to discuss. What trajectory did we need to get on so that we could repeat the process with a good outcome?

While we were meeting with the doctors, they pulled up all the data from every embryo of ours that hadn't survived. For several of them, the placenta sac had formed, but there was no viable... life... no baby was ever conceived. They would've been non-producing embryos. That was a great relief to us.

Laura: I have peace that I didn't lose babies with the fertilized embryos. They never actually would have been viable.

Brian: In theory, they could have picked two different embryos that day for IVF and we might've ended up....

Laura: ...It could've ended up very different. Anyway, all through this process, I'd been learning about fasting. That day, something said to me that I needed to fast. It happened to be on Valentine's Day, so I got up and made breakfast for Brian. I didn't eat. I didn't tell Brian I was fasting because the Bible says not to.

I was looking for my Bible and, for some reason, I couldn't find it. My closet is at the end of our bathroom, so I kept walking back and forth through the bathroom trying to find it. Something kept saying to me, "Take a pregnancy test. Take a pregnancy test."

But I was like, "No, no, no. I'm trying to fast and I'm trying to pray." And it was a *bizarre* thought, I mean I hadn't thought about this before. But this voice said, "You have one test under the sink. Take a pregnancy test."

Still, I was like, "NO! I'm trying to find my Bible so I can pray about stuff." It was almost like, "Leave me alone!"

Brian: But that morning, when we woke up, I'd said, "You're pregnant."

Laura: Yeah, and I had said, "Noooooooo..." There was no way! So anyway, I took the test and this faint little line came up. And I was like, "*What*?!"

Brian: It was one of those tests that has a horizontal line and a vertical line. The vertical line means you're pregnant. The horizontal line is just a control. Well, for some reason, the horizontal line didn't show up; it malfunctioned. But the vertical line was there. So, guess who she called first when she saw the vertical line? The company with the 800 number on the pregnancy test.

Laura: For a good reason...

Brian: …not me, not the doctor…

Laura: … I had to find out!

Brian: They said, "Ma'am, a vertical line means that you're pregnant." But Laura said, "No, no, no. You don't understand."

Laura: I was arguing with the lady. I was thinking, she's just a tech person who answers the phone and she doesn't understand what I'm asking. She's just thinking, *whatever*. So, I dropped the baby off at my in-laws—didn't tell them—and I went to my doctor for a pregnancy test. Well, sure enough, it came back positive.

Brian: The beta hCG was off the charts. They said, "Not only are you pregnant, you are very pregnant." So, while we had been sitting in that doctor's office mapping out our strategy and plotting our course for in vitro in the Fall, she'd been sitting there already four weeks pregnant. We just didn't know it.

Laura: This was on Valentine's Day. Exactly two years prior, we had found out—in the middle of Lowe's—that I was not pregnant. Had you told me on that Valentine's Day, "In two years you will have one baby and find out that you are pregnant with your next," I would have said, I believe God can redeem this time... but will He? Well guess what, He did!

God has mile markers. He doesn't forget. He knows significant dates. The details matter to him, down to specific dates and numbers. He's very aware of what's going on. He cares and He's involved.

So, I didn't have to worry about leftover embryos in the freezer. God knew I was going to get pregnant naturally the second time. He was in control of every single detail.

Brian: And our #3 slipped up on us.

Laura: (laughing) Nursing is not good birth control!

Brian: Our first child was conceived on my birthday. Then, on Valentine's Day two years later, Laura found out she was pregnant with our second one. Then, our third was born on Laura's birthday.

So, within a span of four years, we conceived and delivered three children: one from IVF, two from whatever was broken that God fixed. All on significant dates. So now, people can start praying for the next couple in line. We don't need any more prayers.

Laura: (laughing) Yes, turn it off!

Brian: We made the whole journey from frustration, sadness, uncertainty and worry—everything that you go through—to now having three wonderful, healthy children. And we made more great friends at the church through the group…. Now, when we all get together for birthday parties, you would never guess that our group of friends started over infertility issues.

Laura: We all started off so sad…

Brian: … and now, there are babies everywhere! Some by adoption, some twins, some IVF, some natural. Some, no one knows what worked. There are people who dealt with such agonizing stories….

We all started with the frustration and the questioning, "Is it me? Is it something I've done? What's the problem? Why is this happening?" Now, we all look back and say, "We wouldn't change the experience for anything because we've met some incredible people, and now we can tell our stories to other couples who are struggling."

Laura: You feel this need to help other people. Because when you've been through it, you know how sad they are and how much they're hurting. You want people to know that they're normal for all their feelings….

Brian: People who haven't been through it don't have a clue. They don't understand, they don't know, and you can't describe it. They've heard all the wives' tales and stories and myths and they want to help. So they throw "just relax" at you. We dealt with all that.

You have to have patience and grace with those people. They say things that are hurtful and frustrating, but they don't mean to be. They just don't... they're not....they don't get it. And you can't explain it to someone who hasn't been through it.

You've *got* to connect with people who have been through it. They'll understand. Once you connect, you'll be having conversations—with men, and with women—that you would never have believed you'd have.

Laura: It's so true! I remember going out to lunch with several couples from the group. We got talking about sperm counts, motility, egg quality, cycles, whether it was the right time to go home and try again. I mean... you would **never** have that conversation with most people! But you don't have to apologize or explain yourself. You can just be yourself and talk about what's happening.

Do you believe God had a specific purpose in your infertility experience?

Laura: I truly do believe that I was meant to go through this. It brought me to my knees and I grew so much. As painful as it was, I wouldn't change it.

It was such a growing thing for both of us—for our relationship and our relationship with God—in trusting in His plan and what we were supposed to do. I talk to so many women about it now. I pray for women I meet at the grocery store! I'm so vocal and I feel I was meant to talk to people about it—to give glory to God, and to tell our story.

When I talk to people who are struggling, I tell them that God is working right now behind the scenes. He's working in your marriage, in your finances, in every part of your life—but mainly, what I think I carried away from this experience is that God has a timeline for your child, too. There's a place in history for that child. Just because *we* want something right now and can't wait doesn't mean it should happen that way.

Now, as a parent, I look at my children and see that they're supposed to be influences. God has a plan for their lives. My prayer for my children is that they grow up to be strong Christians. I want them to have a great relationship with God, an even stronger one than me. I want all my children to know that kind of love.

Brian: I learned through this experience that everything doesn't have to happen because *I* make it happen. I just have to be a participant in God's plan. If you are patient, and you have your eyes and ears open, and you pay attention to the people coming into your life, you can have an objective or a destination, but still be relaxed and patient about when and how it happens.

That realization has affected other parts of my life, too. Now, things are moving ahead faster because I'm mindful of whether someone or something is in my life for a purpose.

Laura: I'm very aware of God leading us. Sometimes, I'll say to other people, "I think this may be where God is trying to lead you," and they'll say, "No, no, no." I think…OK, you can take the long way. Enjoy the journey.

Brian: Having gone through all we went through, to now have these three children…. We enjoy them *so* much. It's hard having three under three. We have days that are tiring and frustrating, but I think I'm much more patient and focused on enjoying time with them and spending time with them. That's more valuable than any money or stuff or tangible thing that we might have strived for in the past.

Laura: Now, our life is about family and living to glorify God.

Blessings on You

Finishing our last study together is always bittersweet. Even though lifelong friendships have been formed, we have reached the end of this stage of the journey. So, this meeting is both a hopeful send-off and a sad goodbye.

Every couple longs to move on, toward a future of happy parenthood. But most are still apprehensive about confronting the uncertainty of the future without the security our group represents. Will they be able to hold onto hope? Will their dream ever become a reality? Will their stronger foundations of faith withstand whatever is coming? They must venture forth to find out. That is the key to increasing God-reliance.

All of us will miss the familiarity of this small community. It has created a wall of protection from the world's prying eyes and unsolicited advice. It has provided a safe haven to express dangerous emotions and nurture growing faith. Now, though, it is time to move on—to "break camp" and head once more into the wilderness, equipped with renewed hope and a faith-based expectation that joy awaits.

As we set off on the next part of the journey, we claim Jesus' promise, "If you hold to my teaching, you are really my disciples. Then you will know the truth, and the truth will set you free" [John 8:31-32].

This is the wonderful gift of the time spent in this study—a newfound freedom from the burden of doubting God's purpose. Freedom from constant vulnerability to the obsessive worries of the world. Freedom found in the absolute, eternal truth of God's goodness—which is never held captive by circumstances.

Jesus' words point out one of the few cause-and-effect maxims in all of scripture:" *If* you hold to my teaching... *then* you will know the truth, and the truth will set you free." These words give every couple a road map—through the fallow fields and unfamiliar wilderness, through the periods of waiting and grieving, longing and wondering—to the deeply-desired moment of joy.

They can do the same for you.

So, hold to the teaching you have received. Know the truth. And continue on your way, confident in God's unfailing faithfulness.

"I will pour out My spirit on your offspring,
And My blessing on your descendants.
They will spring up like grass in a meadow,
Like poplar trees by flowing streams."
-Isaiah 44:34

May it be so... to God's delight, and to His glory.

Recommended Resources

One or more of the couples featured in this book recommends the following as a valuable resource for any couple struggling with infertility. These agencies, clinics, websites and books are intended to provide you a starting place—to gather ideas, to research possibilities, to find help and most of all, to nurture hope.

Infertility Support:

RESOLVE (www.resolve.org), the National Infertility Association. This education & advocacy group also serves as an online community-builder for those with infertility. Regional Help Lines provide information on local resources. As of this printing:

➢ Great Lakes Region: Serving Illinois, Indiana, Kentucky, Michigan, Western Pennsylvania, Wisconsin and Ohio. **888.255.1399**

➢ Mid-Atlantic Region: Serving Delaware, Maryland, DC, Virginia and West Virginia. **888.362.4414**

➢ Midwest Region: Serving Minnesota, Missouri, Iowa, Kansas, Nebraska, North Dakota and South Dakota. **888-959-0333**

➢ Mountain Region: Serving Colorado, Idaho, Montana, Utah and Wyoming. **888.592.4449**

➢ New England Region: Serving Connecticut, Massachusetts, Maine, New Hampshire and Rhode Island. **781.890.2225**

➢ Northeast Region: Serving Fairfield County Connecticut, New Jersey, New York, and Eastern Pennsylvania. **888.765.2810**

➢ North Pacific Region: Serving Northern California, Alaska, Hawaii, Oregon and Washington. **888.591.6663**

➢ South Central Region: Serving Arkansas, Louisiana, Texas, New Mexico and Oklahoma. **888-895-6055**

➢ Southeast Region: Serving Alabama, Florida, Georgia, North Carolina, South Carolina, Mississippi, and Tennessee. **888.473.3062**

➢ Southwest Region: Serving Arizona, San Diego, Orange County, Southern California and Nevada. **877.203.7771**

Stephen Ministries (www.stephenministries.org). Stephen Ministers are Christian lay people trained to provide high quality, one-to-one care to individuals experiencing a life crisis. More than 150 denominations offer this service in over 10,000 congregations nationwide. All care is completely confidential and provided free-of-charge. Contact local churches for further information on availability, or visit the website.

Infertility Diagnosis & Treatment:

American Society of Reproductive Medicine (www.asrm.org).This non-profit organization for physicians *and* patients is devoted to advancing knowledge and expertise in the treatment of infertility. Website resources include infertility FAQ, physician referral service, information on clinical trials, and more.

Reproductive Biology Associates (www.RBA-online.com). With 175 cumulative years' experience diagnosing and treating infertility, RBA physicians have facilitated more than 6000 IVF births. Medical Director Dr. Andrew Toledo received the RESOLVE 2009 Hope Award for Advocacy.

Shady Grove Fertility (www.shadygrovefertility.com). A team of 22 subspecialty-trained reproductive endocrinologists, embryologists and geneticists stand behind the clinic's "Shared Risk Program," The program, which draws couples from around the world, provides up to six IVF cycles for a flat fee of $20,000. If a baby is born, Shady Grove Fertility keeps the fee; if all six attempts are unsuccessful, 100% of the fee is refunded.

Yale Fertility Center (www.yalefertilitycenter.org). Close ties with the Yale medical/educational community afford patients ongoing access to research trials and cutting edge techniques, including PGD and ICSI microimplantation. "We do more than provide the latest technologies; we invent them."

Adoption:

Bethany Christian Services (www.bethany.org) is a Christ-centered, not-for-profit adoption agency with more than 75 locations in 32 states, making it the largest adoption agency in the U.S. Last year, more than 1700 children were placed with adoptive families (from within the U.S., as well as international orphanages).

In addition to adoption services, Bethany offers couples access to an infertility ministry called Stepping Stones which sponsors week-end retreats, educational seminars, and more. For further information on adoption, foster parenting, or serving as a temporary "safe family" for families in crisis, visit the website.

Books:

Adopting: Sound Choices, Strong Families
        by Patricia Irwin Johnson
Coming to Term: Uncovering the Truth About Miscarriage
        by Jon Cohen
Empty Cradle, Broken Heart: Surviving the Death of Your Baby
        by Deborah L. Davis
Having Your Baby Through Egg Donation
        by Ellen Sarasohn Glazer & Evelina Weidman Sterling
Moments for Couples Who Long for Children
        by Ginger Garrett & Steve Arterburn
Taking Charge of Your Fertility
        by Toni Weschler
The Complete Adoption Book: Everything You Need to Know
        To Adopt a Child
        by Laura Beauvais-Godwin & Raymond Godwin

Of course, *many* other agencies and resources exist to help you on your journey. If you would like to recommend one that is not listed here (for inclusion in future editions of **Pregnant with Hope**, or for possible use on the website), please let us know. You can visit our website at:

www.PregnantWithHope.com

About the Author

Author Susan Radulovacki is a Stephen Minister and frequent small group leader. She delivers messages of hope and inspiration, along with actionable advice, to infertile couples – and simultaneously equips clergy, friends and family to offer meaningful support.

She developed this series of messages for a unique ministry devoted solely to couples struggling to conceive and to understand God's role in their experience.

Susan earned an MBA from the University of Chicago, where she met her husband, Branko, a clinical psychiatrist and founder of Faith-Works. Together, they are raising two children, both born with the help of reproductive medicine. The four of them enjoy spending family time outdoors and at nearby bookstores.

To find other resources and cause for hope, or to share your story, visit Susan on the Web at:

www.PregnantWithHope.com

Be sure to follow her blog – via RSS feed, Twitter or Facebook – for more insights, inspiration, and words of hope:

www.PregnantWithHope.wordpress.com

Now that you've finished *Pregnant with Hope*, consider using this space to capture your most valuable insights. Ask yourself:

1) What did God teach me through this series of lessons?
2) What did the stories of the ten couples make clear to me?
3) Which of the insights I've gained do I plan to carry forward with me—to the end of our infertility journey, and beyond?

24381757R00132

Made in the USA
Lexington, KY
20 July 2013